中国外语研究学海文丛

人际意义与翻译策略

夏秀芳　著

中国海洋大学出版社

·青岛·

图书在版编目（CIP）数据

人际意义与翻译策略：英文 / 夏秀芳著 . —青岛：
中国海洋大学出版社，2016.8
（中国外语研究学海文丛 / 苗兴伟，蔡金亭总主编）
ISBN 978-7-5670-1232-5

Ⅰ.①人… Ⅱ.①夏… Ⅲ.①英语－翻译－研究
Ⅳ.① H315.9

中国版本图书馆 CIP 数据核字（2016）第 213071 号

出版发行	中国海洋大学出版社
社　　址	青岛市香港东路 23 号　　邮政编码 266071
出版人	杨立敏
网　　址	http://www.ouc-press.com
电子信箱	1922305382@qq.com
订购电话	0532-82032573（传真）
丛书策划	邵成军
责任编辑	邵成军　　　　　　　　　电　　话 0532-85902533
印　　制	蓬莱利华印刷有限公司
版　　次	2016 年 8 月第 1 版
印　　次	2016 年 8 月第 1 次印刷
成品尺寸	144 mm × 215 mm
印　　张	5.375
字　　数	130 千
印　　数	1—1 000
定　　价	20.00 元

总序(一)

General Preface I

近年来,外语语言文学学科的不断发展推动了中国外语研究的繁荣。为了反映最新研究成果和研究动态,中国海洋大学出版社推出了"中国外语研究学海文丛"。本文丛将立足学科前沿,倡导外语研究的科学精神,推出力作,为外语教师和研究者提供一个学术平台和研究阵地,推动外国语言文学学科的发展和繁荣。

外语教师为什么要搞科研? 这似乎是一个不需要回答的问题。一般认为,教学和科研是不分家的。教师在教书育人的过程中经常会遇到各种各样的问题或困惑,有些问题需要通过科研的途径才能找到满意的解决方案。教学与科研之间应该是互为促进、相辅相成的关系。科研不仅是教师职业能力发展的重要组成部分,也是传道授业解惑的重要方面和途径。外语教师如何搞科研? 这既是许多外语教师曾经或者正在思考的问题,也是很多外语教师的困惑所在。在很多人的眼中,外语教师所从事的工作就是教外语,甚至有人把外语看作单纯的工具,认为把教学搞好就行了,没有什么可研究的。持有这种观点的人不在少数。为什么会有人戴着有色眼镜看待外语学科？一方面，有些人的确对外语学科缺乏了解。另一方面，外语学科本身亦有需要我们深思的问题。这些问题表现在以下几个方面：第一，外语教师虽然有接触前沿文献的语言优势，但我们"照着讲"做得多，而"接着讲"做得相对少。近年来，我们在介绍和引进国外理论方面做了很多工作，而在原创性的研究方面还需要加强。第二，外语学科在对接国家战略和重大需求方面做得不够，需要在学术研究上与时俱进，关注社会问题，面向政治、经济、文化、教育和外交领域的国家战略和需求，创新研究思路，提高学术研究的时代性并形成规模效应。第三，外语学科应加强与其他学科的交叉、合作与交流，解决外语与汉语研究的"两张皮"问题，通过学科交叉，开阔研究的视野，并通过学科之间的合作与交流，取长补短，壮大学科研究的实力。

关于如何做科研，这是一个比较复杂的问题。对于研究者来说，从事科研工作需要具备一些基本的修养。具体说来，研究者应具备专门的知识和理论，掌握科学的研究方法，具有一定的研究能力，特别是洞察问题的能力、分析与综合的能力。当然，语言表达能力也是不可忽视的一个重要方面。对于科研本身而言，任何学术研究都离不开研究者对相关文献的深入研读和纵观全局的把握，离不开研究者对问题的独立思考和深刻感悟，更离不开同行之间的学术交流和思想碰撞。总之，学术研究是在科学准则的指导下发现问题和解决问题的心智活动。因此，学术研究中的问题意识是至关重要的。我们不是为了研究而研究，学术研究是受问题驱动的，这就是选题的问题。选题的质量不仅是学术水平的体现，而且是决定研究成果水平的重要因素。怎么才能有高质量的选题呢？研究者除了应具备以上所说的基本修养，还要有问题意识，并且熟悉所从事研究领域的学术动态和学术背景。任何选题都是宏观研究环境的一部分，几乎不存在"前无古人，后无来者"的选题。因此，任何一个选题都会有相关的文献或学术背景，也就是通常所说的"以往的相关研究"。我们在进行学术研究时，需要对已有的相关文献进行处理，这一步骤在论文撰写时通常体现为"文献综述"，是学术论文的一个重要组成部分。文献综述并不仅仅是对以往研究进行描述和总结，而是需要研究者用批判的眼光对相关文献进行分析、归纳和概括。就选题而言，文献综述的目的包括两个方面:(一)对选题进行定位:研究者通过文献综述将自己的选题置于特定的学术背景下，并以此建立选题与已有文献之间的联系。(二)了解研究现状，发现研究空缺:已有哪些研究？以往研究有无缺陷？还有什么需要进一步研究的地方？研究者只有在深入了解研究现状的基础上，才能明确研究方向，突出选题的创新性。这就要求研究者在处理文献时不但要穷尽相关文献,而且要保证文献的真实性和可靠性。

选题时首先需要考虑的问题就是研究的创新性,即选题要新颖。具有创新性的选题应站在学科的前沿,反映学科动态,并在理论和方法上有所创新。创新性体现的是选题的学科价值,包括理论价值和实践价值。我们在选题时需要问:为什么要做这项研究?这项研究要达到的目标是什么?这项研究有什么理论价值和实践价值?总结起来,选题的创新性应包括以下几个方面:(一)理论上,提出新的理论框架,提供新的观点和独到的见解,验证或完善已有的假设或理论,弥补前人研究的不足和局限,或者从新的角度对问题做更深层次的挖掘,赋予新的解释。(二)内容上,选择前人没有研究过的或者学科领域中出现的新问题、新情况,或者为已有的研究提供新的事实。(三)方法上,有不同的分类,采用不同的数据收集方法和分析方法,在研究设计和研究思路上有新的突破,完善已有的方法论。(四)实践上,对教学、翻译、语言使用和文学作品的理解提出新的建议、新的分析和新的方法。如果说得通俗一点,选题的创新性指的是研究中的新问题、新理论、新角度、新方法、新发现。当然能够做到每一点是很困难的,我们能够在某一方面做出创新就可以了,例如,用新的理论或方法解决一个老问题。

就选题的性质而言,有的选题属于描述性研究,研究的主要目的是对现象和事件加以描述;有的选题属于探索性研究,研究的主要目的是满足研究者的好奇心和欲望,回答研究者提出的问题;有的选题则属于解释性研究,研究者基于所建立的概念架构和理论模型对现象加以解释。在选题时,研究者可以根据研究的类型和性质寻找选题的突破口。外语教师在选题时可以考虑从以下几个方面寻找突破口:热点领域、新的理论或视角、悬而未决的问题、被忽视的方面、感兴趣的领域、熟悉的领域、跨学科领域,等等。当然,选题时还需要注意选题的可行性。可行性是研究者能否完成研究的问题,涉及研究者的能力、时间、精力、经费以及研究条件等人力和物力方面的问题。研究者的兴趣与爱好也是制约可行性的重要因素。学术研究需要研究者持之以恒地努力。如果研究者对某一研究领域不感兴趣,其研究也很难持久。

学术研究的最终目的是通过解决学科领域中的问题为人类的知识宝库做出贡献。在我们的学术生涯中,人类的知识宝库为我们的学术研究提供了丰富的营养,使我们能够站在巨人的肩膀上,看得更高,走得更远。"中国外语研究学海文丛"将立足外语学科的前沿,推出最新研究成果,服务外语学科的建设和发展。我们将在选题方面严把质量关,力争以一流的学术成果使"中国外语研究学海文丛"成为名副其实的学术平台和知识宝库。我相信,"中国外语研究学海文丛"

一定会以波澜壮阔之势，推动中国外语研究和外语学科的发展。

苗兴伟

北京师范大学外国语言文学学院

总序（二）

General Preface II

　　中国海洋大学出版社继"外国语言学及应用语言学博士文库"后，于2016年开始推出"中国外语研究学海文丛"，出版外国语言文学一级学科的专著。这是海大出版社重视外语研究的又一重大举措，必将推动我国外语学科的健康发展。

　　长期以来，著书立说是知识分子的重要使命之一，出版专著是每个学者的追求。而撰写专著殊非易事，在某一专业领域如无十年八年的功力，绝无可能。一般来说，专著的诞生要经过几个阶段：从本科或研究生阶段进入某专业领域；在博士阶段及博士后阶段继续学习和研究；围绕某一专题刻苦钻研，发表若干高水平论文；在该领域有所建树，为同行所认可，方可撰写出版专著。从此过程可以看出，真正意义上的专著是以精深的专业知识和独特的学术贡献为基础的。不过，还有一类广义的综述类专著，以回顾梳理前人研究为主，并伴以个人的评论和分析，对初步了解某一领域也有价值。但要深入了解某一领域或专题，还要多读期刊论文和包含个人研究成果的专著。"中国外语研究学海文丛"所包含的主要是此类狭义专著。

"中国外语研究学海文丛"定位是外国语言文学一级学科,是开放性、专业性专著文库,涉及语言学与应用语言学、翻译、文学等方面的研究。这些著作有的是在学位论文基础上修改而成,有的是省部级以上项目的结项报告,有的是作者多年系列研究的整合。但它们的共同点是围绕某一专题,广泛而深入地研读相关文献,找出其存在的问题或空白,通过恰当的研究方法,探究具体的研究内容或回答研究问题,得出有价值的结果和结论。

从事相关研究的学者和正在某个方向学习的研究生,如果花费时间,采取适当的方法选取文丛中的专著进行研读,一定会受益匪浅。在此,我想结合自己的治学心得,谈谈研读专著的方法。首先,要有所选择。受出版界迅速发展的影响,外语研究的专著越来越多。其中,既有外语教学与研究出版社、上海外语教育出版社、北京大学出版社等引进的英语原版著作,也有以上出版社以及科学出版社、上海交通大学出版社、河南大学出版社等出版的国内学者的专著。这些专著涉及外语研究各学科方向,数量可观。面对众多著作,要根据自己的兴趣和研究方向,有所选择。其次,读书要有批判精神。"尽信书,则不如无书。"(《孟子·尽心下》)我们接受的中小学及大学教育,过分强调知识的记忆和吸收,对批判性思维强调和训练不够,导致我们读书时往往认为"书上说的都是对的",不敢有疑问,不会提问题。实际上，学术界没有永远的权威，专著的作者只是在某个领域中对某个专题有较多的了解，先行一步，已经做出了些成绩。当我们用新的理论视角来审视，采用新的研究方法来分析时，很有可能会有新的发现。第三，要详略得当。一般来说，如果对所读内容熟悉，综述部分可以略读，介绍作者自己核心观点或成果的部分则要详读。阅读时要注意思考：作者为什么要研究这方面的内容？采取了什么理论框架？为什么这么做？用了什么研究方法？这种方法有什么优缺点？得出了什么新的发现和结果？作者有没有对其发现和结果做进一步的理论阐释？如果我自己来做这方面研究的话，我会考察哪些相关内容？我会采取什么理论框架与研究方法？我有哪些新理论可以用来解释研究发现？最后，要善于勾连阅读。一本专著提到的相关论文和著作，可以找来阅读，交互印证其中的内容是否正确、方法是否得当。还可以到国内外数据库中查找最近发表的论文，以了解该领域或专题的最新发展，明确是否还有进一步探索的价值。

　　如果广大外语教师和研究生能用正确的方法阅读专著和论文，并身体力行，边教学，边学习，边做研究、写论文，长期坚持下来，一篇篇高质量论文的发表，就如同一粒粒光彩夺目的珍珠的诞生。再假以时日，用统一的思想和框架来贯通这些论文，就可以把这些珍珠串成漂亮的项链，形成学风扎实、论述严谨的专著。

　　海大出版社虽居一隅，但面向全国，以海纳百川的胸怀热情欢迎学海泛舟的学者,以精益求精的编辑质量和强大的发行推广渠道为各位优秀学者的学术精品插上有力的翅膀,让它们飞到广大读者手中。更希望,今日的读者会成长为明天的作者,让我们共同创造我国外语研究灿烂的明天。

蔡金亭

华南理工大学外国语学院

前 言

Foreword

翻译过程是一个复杂的系统，而翻译的复杂性在很大程度上是由意义的复杂性决定的。翻译是不同语言之间意义的传递，所以翻译理论框架必须以意义的研究成果为基础。当今的翻译理论研究，无论是国内还是国外都已经走出了经验式的封闭式宏观描述阶段，对文体的深入研究以及翻译题材和体裁的扩展，促进了翻译理论研究。同时对翻译理论多方面、多角度的探索，也能够加深人们对意义的研究和探索。

翻译理论的研究是以意义为基础的。而功能语法关于意义的论述以全面、系统的特点显示了其科学性。根据功能语言学理论，意义可以分为概念意义、人际意义和语篇意义。功能语言学的特点之一是重视对语境的研究，对这三种意义的研究也是与语境紧密相连的。语境中的语域通过概念意义来表达，语旨通过人际意义来表达，语式通过语篇意义来表达。与其他两种意义相比较，人际意义所涉及的语境更为复杂且不具有系统性。而人际意义却是人们在翻译中容易忽视从而导致翻译不忠实的重要因素。考察一下不尽如人意的翻译作品，很多情况是由于译者没有正确把握和传递人际意义，导致原文和译文在情感上的不对应，读起来总感到难以进入原作的佳境。本书将在研究人际意义各种表达方式的基础上，根据语境理论，进一步探讨不同文体中人际意义的表达方式和翻译策略。

功能语法中的人际意义在书面体中是由语气、情态和语法隐喻来表达的，而笔者在学习和探索中发现，人际意义除了这几种基本的表达方式之外，还有其他多种方式。例如，通过具有感情色彩的词汇可以反映不同的人际意义，各种修辞甚至是句子的长短都具有表达人际意义的功能。

语言学的研究促进了翻译理论的发展。随着语言学理论的进步，尤其是语篇理论的进一步发展，翻译理论界也存在着一种转变，那就是不再盲目追求原文与译文在形式和内容上的对等，而是在研究语境和翻译目的的基础上，探讨不同的翻译模式和翻译策略。翻译的客体是意义，而且这里所说的意义是指使用中的意义，不是死板的语法模式。以此为指导思想，翻译时应该从两个方面入手，其一是满足意义所要求的忠实，其二是满足语言使用环境所要求的可接受性。本书在研究人际意义各种表达方式的基础上，同样将翻译中的语境因素视为影响翻译策略的一个重要方面。本书在前人研究成果的基础上，探讨了语境中的两个层次：

体裁和情景语境,并且研究了这两个层次之间的关系以及在影响翻译策略方面所起到的作用。

在语境理论的基础上,本书探讨了不同文体中人际意义的表达方式,并且以文学文体、科技文体、演讲文体和外贸函电为例,找出各种文体表达人际意义的方式并且进行了比较,找出不同点,以便于译者在翻译过程中在人际意义的理解和传递方面注意文体的特点,选择不同的翻译策略。同时,本书对文体的分析研究还能帮助译者在遣词造句方面更加贴近原文,更好地表达原文意义。

人际意义的主观性决定了它的复杂性。在功能语法的基础上对人际意义各种方式的探索是本书的尝试,将功能语法中人际意义与翻译理论联系起来是本书的立意创新之所在。吸收功能语法理论并且应用到翻译理论领域可以为翻译实践提供理论基础。

目 录

Contents

Chapter 1　Meaning in Context and Nature of Translation

　　 1

1.1　Introduction 1

1.2　Context 2

1.3　Meaning in Functional Perspective 8

1.4　Nature of Translation 10

1.5　Conclusion 18

Chapter 2　Interpersonal Meaning and Translation Strategies 21

2.1　The Mood System of English and Chinese 21

2.2　Translation Strategy on Mood 32

2.3　Modality of English and Chinese 35

2.4　Conclusion 40

Chapter 3　Lexical Ways of Expressing Interpersonal Meaning and Translation Strategy 42

3.1　Introduction 42

3.2 Different Vocative and Translation Strategy·········46

3.3 Different Pronouns and Translation Strategy·········49

3.4 Different Verbs, Nouns and Translation Strategy····51

3.5 Different Adverbs, Adjectives and Translation Strategy
···57

3.6 Exclamation and Translation Strategy ···············58

3.7 Conclusion ··60

Chapter 4 Rhetorical Ways of Interpersonal Meaning and Translation Strategy ·················62

4.1 Introduction ···62

4.2 Translation of Rhetorical Expressions ···············65

4.3 Conclusion ··80

Chapter 5 Typology and the Translation of Interpersonal Meaning ·······································82

5.1 The Influence of Typology on Translation Strategy
···82

5.2 Brief Analysis of Typology and Their Influence on Translation···85

5.3 Conclusion ··97

Chapter 6 Interpersonal Meaning Caused by Gender Differences ····································100

6.1 Introduction ···100

6.2   Male-Female Difference in Their Using Language

  ··· 102

6.3   Some Possible Explanations ·························· 112

6.4   Changes Through Time ····························· 116

6.5   Conclusion ···································· 118

Chapter 7   Appraisal Theory in Functionalism and

       Translation Evaluation ···················· 120

7.1   Introduction ································· 120

7.2   Translation as a Form of Interpersonal Interaction

  ··· 121

7.3   Conclusion ·································· 137

Bibliography································· 141

后　记································· 145

Chapter 1

Meaning in Context and Nature of Translation

1. 1 Introduction

Modern linguistics is characterized by two main directions of research: formalism and functionalism. Formalism focuses on the description of the formal features of language, while functionalism stresses the communicative function of the language form. Scholars who focus on the functions of language tend to make use of the intuitive, non-formal, and non-theoretical generalizations to explain the language facts, and avoid exact formalization. Functionalists try to analyze the base of its form, and the scopes of the interest and concerns of functionalists are much larger than formalists. The study of meaning cannot be satisfactory without the analysis of context. So this section will first explore meaning in context, and then make a study about the strategies of translation. In semantic communication, determined by the factors of context, meanings can be communicated in a "right" and therefore most effective way, or in a "wrong" and therefore ineffective way. If we want to make claims about the "acceptability" of a sentence, a word or word order, etc., we have to appeal to contextual considerations. Since the beginning of the 1970s, linguists have become increasingly aware of the importance of context in the interpretation of sentences.

1.2 Context

1.2.1 *Genre*

There are two levels of context. One is the context of culture, and the other is the context of situation. In order to understand how people use language, we need to consider both the context of culture and the context of situation. For example, we are able to communicate with the sellers when we buy things because we are familiar with what a buying and selling encounter should be like in our culture, the stages such an encounter involves, and the types of language used to achieve the stages. These particular stages are called context of culture, and in linguistics, we use the term "genre". It can be thought of as the general framework that gives purpose to interactions of particular types, adaptable to many specific context of situation that they get used in. Whatever language is being used to achieve a culturally recognized and culturally established purpose, there the genre will be found. Speakers make different lexical-grammatical choices according to the different purposes they want to achieve. For example, the type of words and structures used in a translational genre will not be the same as those used in an exchanging opinion genre. Genres are realized through language, and this process of realizing genre in language is mediated through the realization of register.

1. 2. 2 *Register*

Generic considerations alone are not enough to explain how you identified the sources of the texts. Besides genre, language is mediated through realization of register. To understand what a specific word means, we should refer to the second level of context, context of situation. It is easy to recognize that language usages vary according to the different situations. Through the years, linguistic scholars have explored this field.

1. 2. 3 *Ideas of the Three Functional Linguists*

One of the first researchers to pursue this issue is anthropologist Branislaw Malinowski. Malinowski is distinguished for his semantic theory, in which he illustrates context of situation and emphasizes that the meaning of the word is not related to features of the objects it refers to, but related to its function, that is to say, the meaning of an object is the correct use of the tool. The linguistic events are only interpretable when additional contextual information about the situation and the culture are provided. "Utterance and situation are bound up inextricably with each other and the context of situation is indispensable for the understanding of the words... a word without linguistic context is a mere figment and stands for nothing by itself, so in reality of a spoken living tongue, the utterance has meaning except in the context of situation." (Malinowski, 1946: 307)

One scholar who develops a more general theory of meaning-in-context, influenced by Malinowski, is the linguist of London School, J.R. Firth. Firth considers language as a social and signals, and he holds that the object of linguistics is language in use. According to Firth's view, expressed in an article he wrote in 1935, all linguistics was the study of meaning and all meaning was the function in a context. The mode of experience of people determines the mode of meaning. Firth studies language from a sociological point of view. Here meaning not only means lexical meaning and grammatical meaning, but also meaning in its social context. Firth maintains that the study of meaning is the center of linguistics and that meaning could be viewed in terms of what an utterance is intended to achieve rather than merely the sense of the individual words making up the utterance. Meaning could best be viewed in terms of "functions in context". According to Firth, "What I may call the total meaning of a text is the meaning in situation". (Firth, 1935: 53)

Another very influential figure is M.A.K Halliday whose influence has surpassed that of Firth. He takes over the use of "context of situation" and ultimately develops a sociologically and semantically oriented approach to linguistics. In the late 1950s and early 1960s, Halliday was working on what was then called "scale and category grammar". Since the 1970s, he has been advancing a "systemic-functional grammar" which reveals a much more overtly sociological or what Halliday has called a "social semantics" perspective. Halliday's theory emphasizes the functional aspects of language where language is seen as serving communicative purpose in society, and it emphasizes the intrinsic inter-relationship of language and society. So the study of language must be approached from a fundamentally social point of view. In his "categories of the theory of grammar", he asserts that language has three primary levels: "substance", "form" and "context". "Substance" is the raw material, phonic or graphic; "form" is the organization of this material into meaningful events and context is the relationship of form to the non-linguistic features of the situations in which language operates and to those linguistic features of the situations in which language operates and to those linguistic features not immediately being scrutinized. The major contribution of Halliday's approach to context has been to argue for systematic correlations between the organization of language itself and specific contextual features.

Following the systemic-functional tradition, Halliday also asks which aspects of context are important. He is famous for introducing "register theory" which describes the impact of the immediate context of situation of a language event on the way language is used. According to Halliday, "language varies as its function varies: it differs in different situations. The name given to a variety of a language distinguished according to usage is register". (Halliday, 2000: 132) It is by their formal properties that registers are defined. Halliday further classified field, mode and tenor. Mode is the amount of feedback and role of language; field is the focus of the activity; and tenor is the role relations of power and solidarity. The three factors are related to each other and mutually affect each other. Tenor is perhaps the most crucial factor on regulating the complex relationships between addresser and addressee. Tenor concerns the level of formality of the relation between the participants in the linguistic events. Halliday explains this with the following terms: "The language we use varies according to the level formality, of technicality, and so on. What are the variables under this type of distinction? Essentially, it is the role relationship in the situation in question, such as "who the participants in the communication group are, and in what relationship they stand to each other". (Halliday, 2000: 231) Tenor is closely related to interpersonal meaning, and in translation, it will affect the translation strategy.

1. 2. 4 *The Relation of Genre and Register*

Genre and register are at two different levels of abstraction. Genre can be seen as more abstract, more general than register. One register may be realized through many different genres, and conversely, one genre may be realized through a number of registers. Genres are traditional norms of language in use, each with its own functions and goals adopted by a given community of text users or socio-cultural groups to cater for a particular social occasion. So the features of different genres can be realized according to the context of situation-register. The relationship between genre and register can be expressed in this way: registers impose constrains at the level of discourse structure. Furthermore, genre specifies conditions for the beginning, structuring and ending of a text, and for this reason, genre, unlike registers, can only be realized in completed context. It is the register that confines the use of language directly. The more the analysts know about the features of register, the more likely they are able to predict what is likely to be said and in turn the more he will know how to transfer the meaning in translation. So register is a crucial factor to decide our translation strategy.

1. 3   Meaning in Functional Perspective

Language has formal meaning and context meaning. The formal meaning of an item is its operation in the network of formal relations. The context meaning which is related to extra-textual feature is an extension of the popular and traditional linguistic notion of item in its place in linguistic form. Context meaning is therefore logically dependent on formal meaning. So formal criteria are also important, taking precedence over contextual criteria, and in our study of context meaning, we could not deny the importance of "form". This book will analyze how context affects translation strategy by analyzing how the "form" is transferred into another language.

The previous section has explained the three types of meaning defined by functional grammar. Halliday further suggests that these types of meaning can be related both "upwards" (to context) and downwards (to lexical-grammar). The upward link is that each register variable can be associated with one of these types of meanings. Thus, field is expressed through patterns of experiential meaning in text; mode is expressed through patterns of experiential meaning in text and through textual meaning; tenor is expressed through interpersonal meaning; and these interpersonal meanings are realized through the mood patterns of the grammar.

In order to be clear, functional grammar uses Table 1.1. In fact, the three pairs mutually influence each other.

Table 1. 1　Three Meanings in Functional Grammar

Feature of the context	Functional component of semantic system
Field of discourse (what is going on)	Experiential meaning (transitivity, naming, etc.)
Tenor of discourse (who are taking part)	Interpersonal meaning (mood, modality, person, etc.)
Mode of discourse (role assigned to language)	Textual meaning (mood, modality, person, etc.)

1. 4   Nature of Translation

1. 4. 1   *Equivalence*

All the analysis of meaning serves for the analysis of translation strategy in this book, and now, we turn to the nature of translation. Because of the complexity of the nature of meaning, the definition and nature of translation have also puzzled many who are in and out of this field. For a long time, many scholars have tried to dig into the equivalence in translation, but as we know, translation is a very complex activity, and there is no such thing as equivalence conceived as sameness across languages. Besides, there is always a context in which translation takes place, which influences the decisions that the translators have to make, whereas equivalence is a static, result-oriented concept describing a relationship of "equal value" between two texts or, on lower ranks, between words, phrases, sentences, syntactic structures and so on. So using the static term "equivalence" cannot be satisfactory to describe the requirement of translation.

Because translation cannot reach the equivalence of the source and the target text, the equivalence should not be neglected entirely, either. The previous section has examined meaning, genre, and register, and only on the basis of them, translation theory and practice can be studied scientifically. We all have the ability to predict accurately what language will be appropriated in our own specific context, but in translation which involves two languages, things become different, and the intuition may not work because one of the languages involved is not our native language. This requires us that when we translate, we have to be conscious of the context, and it is the context that helps us make acceptable decisions.

Though it is very difficult to give a satisfactory definition of translation, most translation theorists accept the main point that in translation, it is not word for word but meaning for meaning that we handle with, for words are not clear-cut and distinct entities, and each word normally does not have only one clear and distinct meaning. When we talk or write, we rarely use them in isolation, but use them in a certain environment, and this environment may cause the words to have different meaning from the meaning given by the dictionaries. As the vehicles of communication, words cannot be ignored in the research of translation, but they are not all that we should notice. We should study it in a wider range instead. According to the theories of functional linguistics, we have to study them from the inner side and outer side. What inner side emphasizes is "faithfulness", and what the outer side emphasizes is the "acceptability". It is the interpersonal meaning that is the center of the "acceptability", and if we examine many bad translation works, we will find that the main problem is that the translators pay much attention to the form meaning, but do not pay enough attention to the context meaning, much less to the importance of the interpersonal meaning.

1. 4. 2 *Context and Translation*

Translation theory is not only concerned with the mechanical, lower-level of the linguistic system, but also with higher-order considerations of language in use and text in context. It is not the static entity that we are concerned with, but the wider environment which becomes the key factor to translation practice, understanding of translation work, and even translation teaching.

In his *Translatology*, Huang Long points out that there are three constituent ingredients in the original text: context, form and style. These three are closely interrelated and inseparably interacting. (Huang, 1987: 21-37) The relation between content and form has been discussed by many scholars, and in recent years, style has aroused the interest of linguists and translation theorists. Style is the unity of the comment and the form reflecting the gusto and flavor. It is a complex term under which all kinds of factors, such as textual factors and contextual factors, are involved.

Since translation involves two structures of languages, translators have to deal with the two entirely different forms on the one hand; on the other hand, they should not forget other features bound up with language of the translation, that is to say, the transmission of meaning in translation is determined by the differences of the two languages, the two authors, and the two situations involved. More specifically, translation may deal with different types of works, for example, texts of economy, political essays, technical materials, legal documents and literary works. The text type is at the center of contextual analysis. Translators cannot translate without the study of context, and the translation theory cannot be satisfactory without the analysis of text type. It is clear that the differences in style should be maintained in translation, and the stylistic interpretation is considered as one of the most important aspect of translation analysis in this occasion. In some sense, we can say that style is the meaning. In other words, style is an indispensible part of the message to be conveyed. Translation equivalence, therefore, can be adequately established only in terms of criteria related to text type, and translation theory and practice has been shifted from the concern with equivalence between the source and target texts to the recognition of the need for adaptation to the target situation and purpose.

Style may be seen as the result of motivated choices made by text producers, and it is the different language usages in different situations by particular language users. To analyze different styles, the individual components must be analyzed, which together manifest a certain characteristics. As Levy remarked, "we have to deal with details which are often hardly perceivable, yet are nonetheless significant, since they inform us about the artistic type not by means of themes, composition, or transformation of reality, but by delicate stylistic nuances". Firth also argues this from the angle of meaning, "what I may call the total meaning of a text in situation is broken down and dispensed at a series of levels such as the phonological, the grammatical and the situational levels". (Huang, 1987: 18)

The analysis of translation must accompany the analysis of function, register, and style of the two languages involved. Among many different schools of translation theory, the "Scopes Theory" is the most plausible which considers translation as a form of human interaction and, as such, determined by its purpose or scopes and is the great achievement of Vermeer and Christiana Nord: the founders of the Scopes Theory. In order to achieve a certain purpose in communication, the sender of the message has to choose certain strategies of text production considered appropriate for this purpose. Therefore, in translation practice, the translators should pay enough attention to the context of the original text, the relation between the roles, and the purpose the original text expects to achieve.

In the previous part, this book has pointed out that it is not scientific to use the term "equivalence" in translation and here the Scopes Theory gives another term "adequacy" to displace "equivalence". Compared with the static character of "equivalence", "adequacy" is a dynamic concept related to the process of translation action and referring to the "goal-oriented selection of signs that are considered appropriate for the communicative purpose defined in the translation assignment". (Reiss, 1989: 163) Equivalence at word rank does not imply textual equivalence. The scopes of translation determine the form of equivalence required for an adequate translation. In short, translation theory is conducted on the basis of contrastive linguistics and discourse analysis, and the development of translation theory can also add depth and breadth both to contrastive linguistics and discourse analysis. The following examples show that some lexical ways can express the different interpersonal meaning, and in translation, the translator must use the equivalent words in the target language to express the meaning in the source language. These are examples to show lexical ways of expressing interpersonal meaning and their translation strategy.

The vocatives are a very potent area for the realization of interpersonal meanings, an area very sensitive to these contextual constraints of tenor. Now let's look at the following examples. Although the different ways of vocative represent the same person, it is apparent that they can show quite different interpersonal meanings.

Examples: My dear baby, would you like to stop crying?

My little dear, would you like to stop crying?

My dear, stop crying, please.

Dear, don't cry any more.

Stop crying, son.

Child, stop crying.

John, stop crying.

You little fool, stop crying.

You fool, if you don't' stop crying, I will beat you to death.

In the examples above, all the vocatives refer to the same person "John", that's to say, the ideational meaning is the same, but the communicative effect is quite different. In the first four examples, we can see the tender love of the parent to the child, and from the fifth example to the seventh one, the vocatives have the neutral meaning, but the last two examples show that the parent begins to lose his patience, and man even gets angry at the baby's crying. These examples show that we should use different vocative ways to correspond to different situations.

Translations of the nine sentences should be:

亲爱的宝贝,不要哭了,好吗?

小宝贝,不要哭了,好吗?

宝贝,请不要哭了。

亲爱的,不要哭了。

不要哭了,儿子。

孩子,别哭了。

约翰,别哭了。

小傻瓜,别哭了。

你这个傻瓜,还哭的话我揍死你。

Although the vocatives refer to the same child, the different vocatives express the feeling of the parent clearly. While translating these sentences, translators must imagine the situations where the sentences are said.

Compared with English, Chinese doesn't have tense

or inflection or finite elements. Therefore, we have to use the lexical ways to express meaning expressed by the grammatical ways in English; that is to say, we should often need to add some words when we translate from English to Chinese.

Example: No hard feeling, I said I'm sorry, didn't I?

别生气啦，我不是说对不起了吗？

The two characters " 啦 " and " 吗 " have the feeling of soothing others, which is expressed by the tag question in English.

1.5　Conclusion

Meaning is probably the most complex term in linguistics and because of the complexity of meaning, the nature of translation becomes difficult to define. It has been proved through the history that the theory of meaning in functionalism is more scientific than that of other schools. It divides meaning in three parts and every part has its own system.

In functional linguistics, the study of meaning serves for the analysis of discourse. A successful discourse has to accomplish two tasks: one is to find the right form to express the meaning. As to the interpersonal meaning, it is to choose the suitable ways to express the sentiment or attitude of the speaker or writer. Another is that the choices should be defined by the context factors. The first task is the internal requirement and the second one is external requirement. The theory of functionalism is more scientific than the theory of formalism because it pays more attention to the contextual factors. Translation is closely connected to discourse. Therefore, a successful translation should also accomplish the two tasks: first, it should meet the internal requirement of meaning; second, it should also meet the external requirement of context. Translation is the transmission of language meaning in use. Therefore, the study of translation should adhere to the environment which language is in, and context is one of the crucial factors to decided the translation strategy.

The nature of translation and that of the functional linguistics have some agreements on their attention of context. In recent years, many scholars have applied the theory of functional linguistics to the theory of translation. Theories of functional linguistics can provide scientific bases for translation practice. The study of meaning is closely related to the research of context. One cannot understand the accurate meaning of a sentence without the study of context. Translation can only be conducted on the basis of right understanding of meaning in context. Theorists should explore culture from the aspects of context of culture (genre) and context of situation (register). Based on the ideas of functionalism, translation theorists can explain the term "equivalence" in translation in a more scientific way.

Chapter 2
Interpersonal Meaning and Translation Strategies

2. 1　The Mood System of English and Chinese

There are many ways to express interpersonal meaning both in English and in Chinese. According to the functional grammar, one way of interpersonal meanings of roles and relationships is realized through ways which is called mood.

According to the functional grammar, mood mostly relies on the different types of sentence structure such as declarative or interrogative, the degree of certainty or uncertainty expressed in the usage of modality, the usage of tag questions, vocatives, attitudinal words that either has a positive or negative meaning, expressions to show the degree of intensification, and usages to show various extent of politeness. In functional linguistics, transitivity system is about what is the content of propositions, and mood system is concerned with the approach how that content is presented. Because of the mood system, the relationship between communicative exchanges and grammatical forms can be shown. In this way, when translating, translators will change to the mechanisms which link the highly abstract and universal propositions with the totally physical and context-dependent message or passage.

In the introduction of *Modal Particle of Modern Chinese*, the author points out some characteristics of mood:

(1) Mood indicates the different functions of sentences, and it can express the various sentiments of different communication purpose.

(2) Mood is adhered to the whole sentences.

(3) Mood is a grammatical category, and different kinds of moods can express different grammatical meanings.

In all languages, intonation can express the mood in oral English. Even the words and sentences are the same in written language, different intonations can show quite different meanings. But it is difficult to record vocal sound to prove this. So the paper is going to analyze the diversified forms of written language only. Besides intonation, there are many other ways that have the same function in written language. Let's look at the mood structures of English first.

2. 1. 1 *The Mood System of English*

When we come to look closely at statements and questions of English, we will find that in English they are typically expressed by means of a particular kind of grammatical change, leaving the reminder unaffected.

Halliday, the author of *Brief Introduction to Functional Grammar* gives us the following example. (Halliday, 2000: 36)

Example: The duke's given away that teapot, hasn't he?

　　　　—Oh, has he?

　　　　—Yes, he has.

　　　　—No, he hasn't!

　　　　—I wish he had.

　　　　—He hasn't; but he will.

　　　　—Will he?

　　　　—He might.

In this dialogue, what is happening is that one particular component of the clause is tossed back and forth in a series of rhetorical exchange, and it is this component that carries the argument forward. Meanwhile the reminder, here "away that teapot", is simply left out. In functional grammar, "the component that is bandied about is called mood. The mood structure of the clause refers to the organization of a set of functional constituents. It consists of two parts: (1) the subject, which is a nominal group, and (2) the finite operator, which is part of a verbal group". (Halliday, 2000: 45)

The subject may be any nominal group or pronoun. It supplies the rest of what it takes to form a proposition. The finite element is one of a small number of verbal operators expressing tense by reference to the time of speaking, or modality (*can*, *must*) by reference to the judgment of the speaker. It has the function of making the proposition finite by relating the proposition to its context in the speech event. In some instances, the finite element and the lexical verbs are connected into a complete word, e.g. *loves*, *loved*. This happens when the verb is in simple past or simple present tense, active voice, and positive polarity. In fact, these "fused" tense forms are the two most common forms of the English verb.

The finite verbal operators are listed as follows. (Halliday, 2000: 56)

Table 2. 1   Temporal Operators

	Past	Present	Future
Positive	did, was, had, used to	does, is, has	will, shall, would, should
Negative	didn't, wasn't, hadn't	doesn't, isn't, hasn't	won't, shan't, wouldn't, shouldn't

Table 2. 2   Modal Operator

	Low	Medium	High
Positive	can, may, could, might	will, would, should, is/was to	must, ought to, need, has/had to
Negative	needn't, doesn't/ didn't + need to, have to	won't, wouldn't, shouldn't	mustn't, oughtn't to, can't couldn't mayn't, mightn't hasn't/hadn't

What is ideal is that one typical function is corresponding to one mood structure, and also one structure is corresponding to one typical function, as is listed in Table 2.3.

Table 2. 3   The Relationship Between Typical Function and Mood Structure

Speech function	Typical mood in clause
statement	declarative mood
question	interrogative mood
command	imperative mood
offer	modulated interrogative mood
answer	elliptical declarative mood
acknowledgement	elliptical declarative mood
accept	minor clause
compliance	minor clause

But language is not that simple. There are many other types that do not belong to these columns which are called non-typical clause moods.

Now, let's look at the non-typical clause moods that are often used in Table 2.4.

Table 2. 4　Non-Typical Moods

Speech function	Typical clause mood	Non-typical clause mood
command	imperative	modulated interrogative declarative
offer	modulated interrogative	imperative declarative
statement	declarative	tagged declarative
question	interrogative	modulated declarative

Usually we call the typical mood structure marked structure and call the non-typical mood unmarked structure.

The choice between a marked or an unmarked structure will be influenced by contextual demands. In order to study this field more clearly, we have to explore the connection between clause structure and contextual dimensions.

Examples: Would you like to put it back?

You'd better put it back.

You have to put it back.

Put it back.

All the four sentences have the same function, but they belong to different mood structures. The first three are marked structures. In the first sentence, the command is expressed by an interrogative sentence. This can show the politeness of the speaker. In the second and the third ones, the two statements also have the meaning of command, and the minute difference between the two sentences lies in the different interpersonal meaning of the two verb phrases "had better" and "have to". "Had better" has the meaning of suggestion, but "have to" means it is compulsory. There are many such phrases that can show minute differences, and we will examine them later. The last one is the typical imperative sentence that has the function of command. The above examples show that different mood system may have different interpersonal meanings and indicate the various relationship between the speaker and the listener.

There are many kinds of adjuncts, which can be classified by their meta function, and there are four types of adjuncts that can show the interpersonal meaning. They are mood adjuncts, polarity adjuncts, comment adjuncts and vocative adjuncts.

Mood adjuncts are those that express the speakers' judgment regarding the relevance of the message. There are only two polarity adjuncts: *yes* and *no*. These two types express meanings which are directly related to the mood constituents, but comment adjuncts function to express an assessment about the clause as a whole. They are considered interpersonal elements in the clause, since they add an expression of attitude and evaluation. But because the scopes of comment adjuncts are the entire clause, they should be seen to operate outside the mood structure altogether. Like comment adjuncts, vocative adjuncts do not impact directly on the mood constituent of the clause, but affect the clause as a whole. Therefore, adjuncts also carry the interpersonal meaning. Table 2.5 shows the detailed information of the four types of adjuncts. (Halliday, 2000: 65)

Table 2. 5   Four Types of Adjuncts

	Type	Meaning	Example
Mood adjunct	probability frequency typicality obviousness	how likely how often how typically how obvious	probably perhaps usually sometimes generally regularly of cause, surely
Polarity adjunct	positive negative	yes no	yes no
Comment adjunct	belief admitting persuading request assumption desirability preservation validation evaluating foreseeing	I believe In my opinion I am sure I want you to I think I really hope generally speaking It is true that To be frank I predict that	in my opinion to be honest honestly, believe me please, kindly evidently, no doubt fortunately at first in general wisely, foolishly to my surprise
Vocative adjunct	person's name		John, Mike, George

2.1.2 *The Mood System of Chinese*

Now look at the following examples first.

Examples: 现在去？

现在去吗？

难道现在去？

难道现在去吗？

All the four sentences can express rhetorical mood functioning as interrogation, but they use different ways. In the first sentence, intonation plays the central function; in the second one, the last word can show the rhetorical mood clearly; in the third one, an adverb " 难道 " also plays the same role; in the last sentence, both adverb " 难道 " and modal auxiliary word " 吗 " are used. The examples show that in Chinese, besides intonation, the expressing of mood mainly depends on adverbs and modal auxiliary words. Although the intonation is an important way of expressing mood, the adding of some adverbs and modal auxiliary words will make the sentences much clearer. In addition, the intonation can only express some limited kinds of mood, and it is very hard to transmit the subtle sentiments of the speaker by itself alone.

Like English, there are also four types of mood in Chinese: declarative sentence, question sentence, imperative sentence, exclamatory sentence. Different word order can show different moods and in turn show different interpersonal meanings. Besides word order, some adjuncts can also have clear interpersonal meaning.

This book will use Halliday's modal as the reference to examine the adverbs that can express mood in Chinese.

Table 2.6 shows the comparison of adjuncts in English and Chinese to express mood.

Table 2. 6   Comparison of Adjuncts in English and Chinese to Express Mood

	Type	Meaning	Example
Mood adjunct	probality usuality typicality obviousness	how likely how often how typically how obvious	也许、或许、可能、一定 通常、经常、有时、总是 一般情况、多数情况 很清楚、很显然
Polarity adjunct	positive negative	yes no	是 不是
Comment adjunct	belief admitting persuading request assumption desirability preservation validation evaluating foreseeing	I believe In my opinion I am sure I want you to I think I really hope Generally speaking It is true that To be frank I predict that	我认为、我想、个人观点 坦白来讲 真的、确实是 请、希望 毫无疑问、很显然 令人高兴的是、幸运的是 一般来说、总体来说 奇怪的是 明智地、愚蠢地、错误地 出乎意料地、不出所料地
Vocative adjunct	person's name	Mr. White, Tom	王石青、老王、王教授、王爷爷

Unlike English, Chinese doesn't have finite elements to express mood, but it has modal auxiliary words such as " 啊 ", " 吗 ", " 吧 " or " 呢 " with the same function. In declarative sentences, there is no need to have modal auxiliary words and it is called unremarked mood. In interrogative sentences, we should add " 吗 ", " 呢 ", etc. In imperative sentences, we should use " 吧 " or " 啊 " to express mood, and " 啊 " or " 啦 " can be found in exclamatory sentences.

Examples: declarative: 他是王梅的哥哥。

interrogative: 你是学生吗？

interrogative: 谁在敲门呀？

imperative: 注意啊！比赛马上就要开始了！

exclamatory: 这是多么安静美好的夜晚啊！

The analysis of the mood system of English and Chinese show that both languages can express the interpersonal meaning by different modal adjuncts. So when translating, the translators should try to use the corresponding one to replace the adjuncts in the original. There are still differences between the two systems of the two languages. For example, the finite operators can express the interpersonal meaning in English, but there are no such usages in Chinese. There are modal auxiliary words in Chinese; but there are no such auxiliary words in English. When we translate, sometimes we cannot find the corresponding words, but have to use other ways to translate the meaning.

2. 2　Translation Strategy on Mood

2. 2. 1　*Addition of Auxiliary Modal Words*

Different from English, Chinese doesn't have tense, inflection or finite elements to show the meanings expressed by these grammatical elements in English. Therefore, Chinese has to choose the different Chinese characters to express this kind of meanings. In other words, translators have to add some characters when translating from English to Chinese.

Example: We might just well go the whole hog and stay overnight.

我们索性在这里过夜吧。

"吧" has the meaning of giving a suggestion or asking for the agreement of the listener, and the same meaning is expressed by the word "might" in English.

Example: Don't be angry anymore. I already said I felt deeply sorry, didn't I?

别再生气啦，我不是已经说我很内疚了吗？

"啦" or "吗" has the feeling of making others become calm from angry feeling. In English this meaning is not expressed by words, but by a tag question which is a typical grammatical usage.

Example: We think we have freed our slaves, but we have not. We just call them by a different name.

我们自以为奴隶已经解放了，实际上并没有。我们只不过用一种不同的名字来称呼他们罢了。

The phrase " 罢了 " in Chinese can express the modal meaning of dissatisfaction.

Example: Don't take it seriously. It's only a joke.

不要认真嘛！这只不过是个玩笑而已。

The adding words " 嘛 " and " 而已 " can express the modal meaning in the Chinese translation version.

Like English, there are also non-typical moods in Chinese. For example, the declarative sentence is not telling a statement, but it is a kind of command; an interrogative sentence is not asking a question, but it is used to give kind of information; and there are many other types of marked moods. When we translate these kinds of sentences, we should pay much attention to the real intention of the original, and try our best to transfer the original interpersonal meaning.

Example: Ouch! Isn't that a little steep for a room like this size?

Literal translation: 哎呀！才这么大的一间房,租金不是太贵了吗?

Actually, this is not a question, but a statement. If we change the question into statement when we translate, it should be better.

Examples: Change: 哎呀,才这么大的一间房,房租未免太贵了吧?

Isn't it funny?

Literal translation: 不是很好玩吗?

Change: 真逗!

We shouldn't need very much for a start.

Literal translation: 我们不应该在一开始就需要这么多。

Change: 一开始何必需要这么多呢?

2.2.2 *The Translation of Subjunctive Mood*

Subjunctive mood is an important grammatical category in English, but there is no such corresponding category in Chinese. This needs us to use lexical ways to translate this kind of mood.

Examples: If you finished the job, you wouldn't have said
that.

如果你已经完成这项工作的话，你就不会那
样说了。

If I were you, I'd get up at 5 in order not to miss
the train.

假如我是你的话，我就会在早晨 5 点钟起床
赶火车了。

The subjunctive mood is expressed by tense in
English, but in Chinese, the meaning can be translated using
" 如果……的话 "。

2.3　Modality of English and Chinese

2.3.1　*Modality of English*

Modality is another way of expressing interpersonal
meaning, without which we cannot give a perfect
description of interpersonal meaning. In the modal adjuncts,
the term polarity has been introduced. Polarity is the choice
between the positive and negative. In English, the polarity
is expressed in the element which has both the negative and
the positive usages. However, in reality, besides the two
ends yes and no, there are many other levels which are not

definitely yes or no. There are many intermediate degrees: various kinds of indeterminacy that fall in between. These intermediate degrees, between the positive and negative poles, are known collectively as modality. "Modality is the expression of the speaker's attitude towards what s/he's saying, and it has a close relationship with mood. It is the way the speaker gets into the text: expressing a judgment about the certainty, likelihood, or frequency of something happening or being."(Bassnet, 1998: 76) Modality is an inherently pragmatic phenomenon and it involves many ways in which attitudes can be expressed. Modality should be studied in proposition and in proposal. It may be accomplished by means of modal operators, but it is not necessarily expressed by the modal operators. There are many other ways that have similar function. Adverbs (frankly, seriously, obviously), adjectives (it is probable that, it is certain that) and even prosodic means can be used to express modality.

In functional grammar, there are two main types of modality. The first type is the modality expressed in proposition, and the second type is the modality in proposal. "In proposition, there are two kinds of intermediate possibilities: (1) degree of probability: possible/probably/certainly; (2) degree of usuality: sometimes/usually/

always."(Hallidy, 2000: 125) Halliday uses the term "modalization" to refer them.

If the speaker chooses to express modalization, this may be achieved grammatically in the following three ways: "(1) by a finite modal operator in the verbal group; (2) by a modal adjunct of probability and usuality; (3) by both."(Halliday, 2000: 138)

In proposals, there are also two types of intermediate possibility depending on the speech function, whether command or offer. (1) In a command, the intermediate points represent degrees of obligation. (2) In an offer, they represent degrees of inclination. Halliday refers these two types as modulation.

Examples: They must have known.

They certainly knew.

They certainly must have known.

It must happen.

It always happens.

It must always happen.

You must be patient.

You are required to be patient.

I must win.

I'm determined to win.

As far as we have been concerned, the finite modal operators and the modal adjuncts have already been covered. There is another word that can function as modal adjunct, and that is the word "not". In this case, it is phonological salient and may also be tonic. Because it belongs to the function of prosodic feature, it will not be examined in detail in this book.

Example: We were /not im/pressed.

2.3.2 *Modality of Chinese*

The modality of English can be expressed by modal operators: can, could, may, might, must, shall, should, will, would, ought to, used to, need, dare, have to, and modal adjuncts or by both. In Chinese, there are no operators and the modality is expressed by these words: 能, 能够, 会, 可以, 敢, 愿意, 肯, 要, 得, 应该, 应当, 该, etc. These words have similarity with the modal operators when used to express the interpersonal meaning.

Examples: 你能解决这个问题。能
他们肯定会通知老师的。肯定
硬让我去，一定得捅出乱子来。一定得
你这样自以为是是要栽跟头的。要
这种事经常发生。经常
这种事不应该经常发生。不应该经常

你<u>得</u>常回家看看。<u>得</u>

我<u>愿意</u>到高校当老师。<u>愿意</u>

2.3.3 *The Translation Strategy of Modality*

The section above of this book has analyzed the two systems of modality in Chinese and English, and the two systems show that there are a lot of differences between the two languages. Therefore, the translation of the modality is not simply to find the corresponding words of the original language, but to understand the meaning of the original modal operators of English and the *nengyuan* (能愿) words in Chinese, then to find a proper way to translate the interpersonal meaning.

Examples: If I didn't walk every day, I should expired.

我一天不散步就会断气。

You ought to go and try the department in downtown. They may have some right ties to go with your suit.

你应该去市区的百货公司看看，他们可能有配你的西服的领带。

He might pay us. He is quite well off now.

他也该还我们钱了，他现在已经相当富裕了。

Her trip to Latin America may offend some 19th

century chauvinists but the first lady's striking a blow for the full partnership of women.

这位第一夫人的拉美之行也许会触犯某些 19 世纪式大男子主义者,但她的这次出访是为妇女的充分参政打出了有力的一击。

2.4 Conclusion

To grasp the meaning of the original language is the first step in translating. Interpersonal meaning is one of the key points in understanding the meaning of the original language. This chapter examined the different expressions of interpersonal in English and Chinese, including the different system of mood and modality in both languages. Based on the analysis, this chapter examined the translation strategies, especially the strategies about the interpersonal meaning.

All the modal operators in these examples are translated into *nengyuan* words in Chinese. However, because of the two different systems, *nengyuan* words in Chinese cannot fully express the subtle differences of the original. For example, in English, the three modal operators, must, ought to and should, have minute difference: the meaning of "ought to" is stronger than "should", and both "ought to" and "should" emphasize the objective meaning, but "must" emphases the subjunctive meaning. This minute difference is difficult to translate into Chinese because there is no corresponding usage in Chinese. So this requires the translators to choose different words and use lexical ways to transfer the subtle meaning.

Actually, vocatives, pronouns, verbs, nouns and adjectives can also carry the interpersonal meaning. For example, you may use some words that can show your politeness and respect when you talk to your professor or someone who has the higher rank, but you will use a totally different vocabulary if you talk to your best friends.

Chapter 3

Lexical Ways of Expressing Interpersonal Meaning and Translation Strategy

3. 1　Introduction

Language is a tool, but it has the special characteristics compared with other ordinary tools. Language is not created by man deliberately. It is a social and historical development, entails a very complicated series of human activities, but it is not a finite system. Through the study of linguistics, many of the studies deal with the field of meaning, but the complexity of language made this field very hard to give an explanation.

Because communication between people, groups, nations or other social organizations becomes more and more important, the need to study meaning of language becomes even more pressing. The study of meaning concerns many fields. So considering just one field in the study of meaning is not enough. Philosophy, psychology and linguistics all claim a deep interest in the study of meaning. Therefore, if semantics is defined as the study of meaning, there will be many different, but intersecting branches of semantics.

Existence and cognition are the most important pairs in philosophy. At first, meaning was interpreted from the dimension of existence. Matin (2003) argues that the limitation of early theories is that they consider language as being static and isolated and study the meaning of language mechanically, without paying enough attention to the different factors and variations that emerged in human beings everyday life. Generally speaking, these theories tend to study language within the scope of grammar and logic and insist to get rid of the elements that are concerned with psychology. They did not realize that as a social phenomena that is closely related to human activity, language develops as the society develops. Therefore, no one can study meaning without considering the practice of human being in which language is used.

With the development of philosophy, meaning was understood from the dimension of cognition; that is, people began to associate meaning with human mind. The famous "semantics triangles" of Ogden and Richards shows a great improvement in the interpretation of meaning and shows that the psychological factors began to attract people's attention. In the triangle, the symbol of a word that signifies "things" by virtue of the "concept" associates with the form of word in the minds of the speaker of the language.

Later, meaning was understood from a wider dimension and the study from a context point of view came out. This study is based on the presumption by Halliday (1985) that one can derive meaning from or reduce it to observable context. The famous formula of Bloomfield, which is the representative mark of behavioral school, clearly points out the importance of the situation in which the speaker utters. Bloomfield argues that if there is no situation, the response will not happen, and this is the function of context. In various contexts, or in various registers in a more narrow sense, language may have different meanings and functions. For example, speaker may use language to persuade, to inform, to ask or to invite. According to functional grammar, the meaning is classified into three types: experiential, interpersonal and textual functions.

Experiential meaning is the meaning about how people represent experience in language. Interpersonal meaning is a strand of meaning that is running throughout the text and expresses the writer's attitude towards the subject matter. Finally, while expressing both experiential and interpersonal meaning, a text also makes what we describe as textual meaning. Textual meaning refers to the way a text is organized as a piece of writing. Halliday (2000) claims that a text can make these different meanings because units of language are simultaneously making three kinds of meaning.

Translation is the transfer of meaning from one language to another. In order to transfer the meaning exactly, the translator has to master the meaning in context. This book will explore the lexical ways of translation of interpersonal meaning in context. During the translation process, readers always expect omniscient translators to have an ideal translation version, judged by the stands of equivalence put forward by Eugene Nida (1991). The concept of "equivalence" is not clear and cannot be applied to translation or interpretation today. In today's translation theory, "adequacy" is a criterion used to judge whether the translation is acceptable or not.

The systems of modality in Chinese and English are different. Therefore, the translation of the modality is not simply to find the corresponding words of the original language, but to understand the meaning of the original modal operators of English and the *nengyuan* words in Chinese, then to find a right way to translate the interpersonal meaning.

3. 2 Different Vocative and Translation Strategy

The vocatives are a very potent area for the realization of interpersonal meanings, an area very sensitive to these contextual constraints of tenor. Now let's look at the following examples. Although the different ways of vocative represent the same person, it is apparent that they can show quite different interpersonal meaning.

Examples: My dear son, would you like to finish your homework?

My darling, would you like to finish your homework?

Sweetheart, it is time to finish your homework, please.

Dear, finish your homework.

Finish your homework, son.

Child, finish your homework.

Mike, finish your homework.

You little fool, go to finish your homework.

You fool, if you don't finish your homework, I will punish you severely.

In the above examples, all the vocatives refer to the same boy; that is to say, the ideational meaning is the same, but the communication effect is quite different. In the first four examples, readers or listeners can sense the tender affection of the parent to the boy, and from the fifth example to the seventh one, the addressing has no tender love nor scolding, which is the neutral meaning, but the last two examples show that the parent starts to get angry and his patience is running out. In order to show the subtle difference of the addressing, the translation of these vocatives should also express these differences.

Now, let's examine some examples of Chinese to see how vocatives affect the interpersonal meaning of the sentence.

Examples: 老伙计! 最近怎样?

这关系到企业的生死存亡, 张总!

还有呢, 哥哥, 这是总部首长叫我送给您的。

In the first example, the vocative shows the close relationship between the speaker and the listener. In the second example, the vocative has the meaning of eagerness to persuade the person who is called, and in the third one, the vocative can attract the attention of the listener, and it tells the listener that what the speaker is going to say is very important.

The big difference between English and Chinese on the point of vocative is that Chinese vocatives often have modal auxiliary words after them.

Examples: 老张啊,斗争很复杂! 咱们可不能稍微打个 盹儿,更不能当唐僧。

明天天亮……儿呀……你……就要离开娘!

儿呀儿呀,你听那催命的更鼓三声响,儿呀儿 呀,为娘恨不能替代我儿赴刑场。

周总理啊,周总理,全国人民都在哀悼您,都 在呼唤您,都在想念您。

In the first example, the modal auxiliary word after the vocative shows that the speaker says these words after deep thinking and he really hopes that the listener will listen to his persuasion.

In the second one, the continuous using of vocatives and modal auxiliary words shows the agony and frustration of the mother when her son will be sentenced to death by the enemy.

Usually when the speaker uses vocatives, the person who is called can be seen when the speaker talks, but the last example is different from the other examples because the person called is not present. In this sentence, the vocative and the modal auxiliary word "啊" can still show the deep sorrow of people on losing their beloved premier.

Because the vocative can show the strong interpersonal meaning, translators have to grasp this sentiment and transfer it into another language with vocative or other lexical ways.

Example: "I don't have to tell you anything, Norman Page, not a single thing." She said.

The person who is talking is the lover of Norman Page. Usually she only calls him Norman, and now the vocative shows that she is very angry. Besides this vocative, an adjunct "愤愤地说" can be used.

Example: "我不需要告诉你任何事情，诺曼·佩奇，任何事情都不需要。"她愤愤地说。

3.3 Different Pronouns and Translation Strategy

The different usages of the pronouns can also show the different interpersonal meanings, although in modern English, there is no difference of "tous" and "vous" as in French, and similarly difference of "您" and "你" in Chinese. The use of "we" can also show the different interpersonal meaning in various situations. Let's examine the following examples.

Examples: We are going to spend the winter vacation in the Hainan Island.

我们明天开始放假，你们呢？

This is the usual usage of the pronoun "we". Here "we" indicates the meaning of the party of the speaker side, which is the opposite side of the listener in the conversation. Let's examine the following example.

Example: Shall we sit there and have a talk, John?

明天我们去爬山吧。

Different from the first example, here "we" includes the speaker and the listener. It is clear that the speaker wants to sit to have a talk, and he wants to ask the idea of the listener. Here the pronoun "we" is used to indicate that there is little distance between the speaker and the listener. In the fourth example, the speaker wants to climb the mountain the next day, and he asks if the listener also wants to go with him. In order to show the close relationship with the listener, he uses " 我们 " instead of " 你 ".

Examples: Now, we must be a good boy, and stop crying.

老师对学生说："我们必须遵守纪律，好好学习。"

Different from the above examples, here the pronouns "we" and "我们" have quite different meanings from the traditional meaning of "we". It only represents the listener without including the speaker. This kind of usage may be found especially in the case of speaking to children and to patients. "We" indicates the meaning of persuasion or consolation, and when the listener hears the pronoun, he may have a feeling of comfort and he will have the feeling that there is little distance between the speaker and him. In this way, a friendship may be easily established.

The choice of the pronouns can clearly show the feeling of the speaker or writer. It is an important way to express the minute sentiment. Translators should catch this interpersonal meaning in its context expressed by the pronouns, and transfer the meaning in a corresponding context in another language.

3.4 Different Verbs, Nouns and Translation Strategy

Aside from vocatives and pronouns, there are many other very significant ways in which these dimensions of tenor impact on language usage can be found. Different choices of verbs, nouns, adverbs and adjectives can also show the different attitudes of the speaker or writer. Readers can find the different verbs in the following examples.

Examples: No matter how you sing highly about him, I <u>still</u>
<u>dislike</u> him.

I <u>hate</u> mice!

I really <u>appreciate</u> of your coming despite the
hostile weather.

Everyone <u>loves</u> his motherland.

All these sentences clearly show the different attitudes
of the speaker because of the meaning of these verbs. In
the first two examples, the speaker shows the negative
interpersonal meaning because the meanings of the verbs
are derogatory, and in the last two examples, the meanings
are commendatory. These examples tell us that the different
choices of verbs have the function of expressing the
interpersonal meaning.

There is another type of showing interpersonal
meaning by using verbs. In this case, the verbs have the
same ideational meaning, but the connotative meaning is
different, which also has the function of expressing different
attitudes of the speaker.

Let's see the following examples.

Examples: His grandfather died a martyr's death in the
revolutionary war.

John's father has passed away before he went to school.

Alice died in a car accident.

That old guy has kicked the bucket.

Although the four expressions have the same meaning of "death", they should be used in different situations to show different interpersonal meanings. In the first two examples, the two phrases show the respect to the people who died, and in the third one, "die" has the neutral meaning, but in the last example, the phrase can show that the person who died is not important at all and the speaker does not show any sorry to his death.

The above eight examples show the two kinds of verbs that have the function of expressing interpersonal meaning: one way is using the original meaning of the verbs, and another way is using the different connotative meaning of the verbs or verb phrases.

Similarly, the different choices of nouns can also express interpersonal meaning. Let's examine the following example.

Example: I consider her a very special soul and I know the world misses her.

Here Richard Carpenter, the singer of "Yesterday Once

More", recalled her sister Karen Carpenter with the feeling of love, respect and regret. Let's examine the following example.

Example: His principle virtue is his honesty.

When readers see the word "virtue", they will have a kind of positive feeling because the noun itself carries the interpersonal meaning. Let's examine the following example.

Example: The accident victims were taken to hospital.

The word "victim" can clearly show the sympathetic feeling of the speaker. Let's examine the following example.

Example: What a mess you have made!

The word "mess" bears the meaning of dissatisfaction of the speaker towards the listener. Let's examine the following example.

Example: You are really a troublemaker.

The word "troublemaker" has the negative meaning, and can express the anger of the speaker.

Since the verbs and nouns can express the attitudes of the writer or speaker, translators have to find out the degree of the attitude, and use the most suitable word to transfer the meaning. If the original language is positive, translators have to find the positive words to translate. If the original language is negative, translators have to find the negative words to translate. If the original language is neutral, translator should not use any word that shows the positive or negative meaning. Let's examine the following example.

Example: So very much money—well over $400 billion a year—is tossed around by the federal government that is not surprised that some of it is spent foolishly.

Original Translation： 联邦政府既然每年能将远远超过 4 000 亿美元的巨款随随便便地花掉,那么其中有些钱花得愚蠢就不足为奇了。

As we know $400 billion is a great amount of money, so the original sentence is showing an attitude of surprise and anger. However, the Chinese version "随随便便地花掉" cannot express the angry feeling. Now we change the translation into the following version.

Changed Translation： 联邦政府既然每年能将远远超过 4 000 亿美元的巨款挥霍掉,那么其中有些钱花得很愚蠢就不足为奇了。

In the new version, the word "挥霍" can express the anger of the speaker, but "随随便便地花掉" cannot express the degree of anger and dissatisfaction. Let's examine the following example.

Example: "My daughter Mallika is studying sociology at Stella Maris. She is just like you, an innocent baby."

Original Translation: "我女儿麦莉卡在斯德拉·马里斯攻读社会学，她跟你一样，是个天真的孩子。"

In the original sentence, the mother uses the word "baby" but not "girl" when referring to her daughter, which shows the tender love to her child. However, "孩子" cannot express this subtle sentiment in the translation version. This example shows that the nouns can carry interpersonal meaning. When translating, translators should also pay attention to the minute difference of the meanings of different words. As to this example, it can be changed into the following one.

Changed Translation: "我女儿麦莉卡在斯德拉·马里斯攻读社会学，她跟你一样，是个天真的小娃娃。"

Let's examine another example.

Example: Without the bureaucracy, the relations with other nations would be difficult to maintain; international trade would become unpredictable.

The word "bureaucracy" often has the derogatory meaning " 官僚作风 ", but in this sentence, readers should notice that it has the commendatory meaning, talking about the positive function of government. So in translation, translators have to choose a corresponding word to express this meaning. Now the sentence can be translated into:

如果没有政府机构,与外国的友好关系就很难保持;国家间的贸易情况也将无法预料。

3.5 Different Adverbs, Adjectives and Translation Strategy

Adverbs and adjectives are used to stress or reduce the degree of verbs and nouns. So they tend to express the kind of feeling or emotion of the speaker or writer. When translating, translators have to find the appropriate words to transfer the same meaning. Here translators should remember that to show the original interpersonal meaning, they don't need to translate the words to the same type all the time. The change of word type can also express the meaning more accurately.

Example: 我们几姊弟和几个小丫头都很喜欢——买种
的买种,动土的动土,灌园的灌园;过不了几
个月,居然收获了。

My brother, sister and I were all delighted
and so were the young housemaids. And then
some went to buy seeds, some began to dig the
ground and others watered it and, in a couple of
months, we have a harvest!

In this translation, the original adverb "居然" in
Chinese version means *unexpectedly* or *surprisingly*. If
we use these adverbs to translate, it is loyal to the original
version and it is acceptable, but this translation version uses
only one conjunction "and". This conjunction connects
the meaning of the sentences naturally and expresses the
interpersonal meaning delicately.

3.6   Exclamation and Translation Strategy

In conversations, especially in informal conversation,
people often use mood words to show his/her feeling.

Examples: Well, I'm going to be his mother now. 嗯,现在
我就是他的妈妈了。

So, um, what are you gonna call it? 那么,嗯,

你叫它什么？

Shh, don't tell the kid like that. 嘘，不要和孩子那么说。

Ah, it's right behind you. 啊，他就在你后面。

Uh? Piranha! Wow! 唔？食人鱼！啊！

Oh, I bet you will. 哦，你一定会的。

Oh, Jane, oh, thank goodness. 哦，简，哦，谢天谢地。

Good heavens! What happened? 老天，发生了什么事？

Oh boy ... 哦，天啊……

It is not the baronet, it is, why, it is my neighbor, the convict. 这不是准男爵，这是，啊，这是我的邻居，那个逃犯！

Aha! I've caught you at last! 啊哈！我可抓住你了。

There, there! don't cry! 好啦，好啦，别哭了。

Grasping the sentiment of the exclamation in the original context is the first step to translate it into another. The first important step is to find out whether they are expressing the meaning of surprise, happiness or disappointment from their context. Both in English and Chinese, there are a lot of exclamatory words that can express minute difference in their sentiment, and it is very difficult to translate them into another language without considering the context factors. In order to catch the meaning of the original language, translators need to study them in their context, and it is from the context that translators can decide which word to choose.

Examples: Ah! You're back in time.

啊！你们按时回来了！

Here "ah" shows a feeling of gladness.

Ah! Never have I heard of such a Mr. Green.

哟！这样一位格林先生我可从来未听说过。

Here "ah" shows a feeling of surprise.

The same exclamation word "ah" is translated into different words in Chinese, which is determined by their context.

3. 7 Conclusion

In translation, the study of meaning is the key factor. In the case of the unsatisfying translation version, usually the interpersonal meaning is not transferred probably. This chapter first explored the different usages to express mood and modality in English and Chinese, and then it studies mainly the lexical ways of expressing interpersonal meaning and translation strategy between English and

Chinese. On the basis of this comparison, this chapter tries to summarize the strategies in translation to use lexical ways to express interpersonal meaning.

In the process of translation, translators have to consider the higher levels involving entire texts in situational, social, and cultural context, and besides these, lower linguistics levels involving sentences, words and phrases should also be taken into consideration. According to Newmark (1981), theories based on functional linguistics have major implications for thinking that good translation should consider factors at all levels. The functional school is mostly concerned with the establishment of what context factors translators should be aware of and what guidelines they should follow. Reiss (1989) emphases the basic competences and the overall perspectives from which translators should view assignments. Translators should be aware of the context factors in all levels before they undertake an assignment.

Chapter 4

Rhetorical Ways of Interpersonal Meaning and Translation Strategy

4.1 Introduction

4.1.1 *Rhetorical Ways in Communication*

Rhetoric began in ancient Greece two thousand years ago. It is a science in studying language. Rhetoric chooses the expressive ways in communication according to different situations. In daily interactions and all kinds of written texts, people use many sorts of rhetorical ways to express their meaning in a vivid way, which gives the listeners or the readers a deep impression. Rhetoric, to a great degree, determines whether the speaker is eloquent or the writer is versatile. Both English and Chinese have been researching and improving the art of using language, and each of them has a unique set of rhetoric. The rhetorical expressions in both languages share some similarities and differences. Most of the expressions in English can find similar or equivalent expressions in Chinese. But rhetorical expressions often show the features of source language which cannot easily be translated into the target language. Because of the different history, geography, tradition and living environment, people in different countries may choose different ways to express the same idea or concept. In translation, for these kinds of untranslatable expressions, translators have to translate in a flexible way. Sometimes, the forms of the original language cannot be retained in order to translate the meaning. In other words, it is quite difficult to translate meaning and form at the same time in the field of rhetorical usages.

4.1.2   *Translation and the Criteria of Translation Works*

Translation plays a very important role in cultural communication and international trade. It is also vitally important in the spreading of religious beliefs. To decide whether it is an ideal translation, the following factors are often considered. First, whether the translation is accurate. The meaning should be the same or as close as possible to the source language. Second, whether it is natural. The translation version should use the natural forms in the target language. Readers of the translation version can have the natural feeling as reading the works of its own language. The third is communicative. The translation version should express all aspects of the meaning in the source language. (Bassnett, 1980)

Translation involves a lot of factors including the features of the two languages, the language competence of the translators and the situation in which the translation takes place. Translation can never be an easy transfer of words from the source language to the target language. (Catford, 1965) The quite different language systems may add difficulty in the translation process. There are many kinds of translation modes, such as oral to oral translation, written to written translation, translation with pictures. Whatever the mode, translation is always a dynamic process, and the translation products are different from different translators. For two thousand years, translation theory has been concerned mostly with literary or religious works. No matter what kind of translation, a satisfactory translation is possible, but in most cases, an ideal translation is so hard to accomplish due to the extremely complicated factors of interlingual communication. For the last forty years, with the development of science of translation, theories about the translation of general language began to be emphasized. (Hatim, 2000) The study of this paper is to summarize the rules of the rhetorical expressions in English and Chinese from the linguistic point of view, and then apply them in translation practice. In order to provide useful translation tips, some of the features that can be summarized should be declared in a definite way.

4. 2　Translation of Rhetorical Expressions

4. 2. 1　*Translation of Metaphor*

The study of metaphor has aroused the interest of many scholars, but the study of metaphor has been neglected in translation theory. In recent years, some scholars argue about if metaphor could be translated due to the different thinking modes of the two language systems. The biggest problem that hinders the translation of metaphor is that different cultures have concepts and symbols in varying ways, and the metaphors are usually culture-specific. For example, in the sentence "She is a cat", the sense is spiteful and evil in English, whereas in German, a cat is not associated with spitefulness or evil but with grace and elegance. So the literary translation from English into German would not communicate the metaphorical meaning. Another example shows that some metaphorical meaning in German cannot find the equivalence in English.

"Sie ist eine alte Ziege" expresses a blend of stupidity and unpleasantness in German. However, the negative meaning is not associated with goat nor cat in English. So as to the translation of metaphor, as Newmark puts it, "a new truth is created that requires a suspension of disbelief, a fusion of perception and imagination". (Newmark, 1985: 296) The concept of "new" relies greatly on the metaphor itself. During the process of translation, it is often not so easy to keep the original form; that is to say, the formal equivalence is not easily maintained to transfer the same meaning. Otherwise it could provoke misunderstanding to the readers or audience of the target language. Dynamic equivalence is defined as a translation principle using various approaches to transfer the meaning instead of translating literally. Dynamic equivalence can obtain the same impact to the target readers as the one aroused in the source language. So dynamic equivalence has been favored by many translation theorists as the expressions are more understandable.

Another sense of metaphor that has to be mentioned is the fading metaphor, which is the result of lexicalizaion from the familiar quote. Some theorists argue that among the types of metaphors, the more bolder and more creative the metaphor, the easier it is to translate in other languages. Some severely criticize this, claiming that all metaphors should be translated literally. As for whether a metaphor could be translated, Mary Snell-hornby says "whether a metaphor is translatable means whether a literal translation could recreate identical dimension. How difficult it is to translate, how it can be translated and whether it should be translated at all cannot be decided by a set of abstract rules, but must depend on the structure and function of the particular metaphor within the text concerned." (Mary, 2001: 58)

Example: She was born with a silver spoon in her mouth.

The phrase "silver spoon" means that she was born into a rich family. The expression may be different in another language, but has the similar meaning. In this case, we can choose the public-accepted usages, instead of changing its form in order to get the equivalence in the source language. In Chinese, there is one expression " 含着金钥匙出生 " that can equally describe this meaning. So the translation will be " 她是含着金钥匙出生的 ".

A great amount of linguistic or extra-linguistic factors will influence the appropriate equivalence in a given context. (Steiner, 2001)

On the lexical level, the words and expressions in their situations are sometimes called lexical sets. Sometimes there is no direct equivalence for a term in the target language. Or the target language has the similar concept, but there is no such appropriate words. Or sometimes the concept in the source language may not have the same idea in the target language.

Translators have to use strategies to solve the problem. One way that is frequently used is to translate the source language by a more general word. The opposite way is to translate the original language by a more neutral word with less expressive meaning. In these two ways, the meaning is not transferred truthfully. So the translators need to have some notes to give some explanation.

In some cases, translators will choose to use a culture-characteristic component or expression with a term in the target language which does not have the exact propositional meaning, but the term will probable cause a similar reaction in the target language.

Another way of solving this problem is to paraphrase using a related word, in the case when the idea expressed by the source language is lexicalized in the target language, but in a different way.

Using a loan word with some explanation can also solve the problem. This way is particularly common when translating culture-specific items. When a word in a text is repeated several times and there is no equivalent term in the target language, it is useful in using a loan word and it can be used later in the translation.

4. 2. 2   *Translation of Simile*

Simile uses the similarity between the object and the vehicle. In English, "like" and "as" are often used to show this kind of rhetorical expression. Using some other easily-understood expressions will create a vivid impression.

Example: Cool as a mountain stream! Cool as fresh Consulate.

This is the advertisement of cigarette Consulate. This kind of cigarettes add mint to tobacco, which makes a cool taste. So the advertisement uses a mountain stream to show the taste. When translating, translators can translate it literally as follows.

凉如高山流水，爽似康斯丽特。

The Chinese version keeps the original simile "a mountain stream". The word "高山流水" gives consumers a cool and fresh sense. This kind of expression will arouse the interest of readers and the translation not only keeps the original meaning, but also expresses the meaning.

Another example is the sentence to talk about the

comfort of shoes for children. It says, *"They are as soft as mother's hands"*. It can be translated literally as " 像妈妈的手一样柔软 ".

4. 2. 3 *Translation of Parenthesis*

Parenthesis is isolated from other grammatical elements, but it has the close relationship with the whole sentence. Parenthesis has the meaning of calculation, guessing or showing attitude of the speaker. Parenthesis is often put at the beginning or in the middle of the sentence. Between the parenthesis and other grammatical elements, there are usually prosodic pauses. Usually parenthesis is used to stress or relax the intension, and sometimes, it may have very strong interpersonal meaning.

Example: 你听我说，我说这话绝对是为你好！

The parenthesis " 你听我说 " is put at the beginning of the sentence to show the leisure of the speaker, and it can also attract the attention of the listener. Parenthesis shows strong emotion of the speaker or writer. The interpersonal meaning in this kind of rhetoric is clear, and the translation version should express the same functional meaning.

Example: The peasant woman receives nothing since whatever she earns is the property—as she herself is—of the husband who has brought her as his wife.

The parenthesis "as she herself is" emphasizes that the peasant woman has nothing, and even herself doesn't belong to her.

Usually the parenthesis in the original sentences is also translated into the same kind of parenthesis in the target language.

4. 2. 4   *Translation of Climax*

When people arrange elements of language, they tend to be guided by their degree; that is, they will list their degrees from small to big, light to heavy, low to high, and slowly get to the climax. This arrangement can make the language well-balanced. The rhetorical method is often used in speech and argumentation, which can make the speech and the view of the argumentation powerful.

In climax, the choice of words is very important to show the degree, which makes the effect of rhetoric. The degree can arouse a kind of emotion in listeners or readers.

In order to express the original interpersonal meaning, translators have to understand the original meaning and keep the climax structure in the translation. Usually the climax shows that the meaning is becoming stronger and stronger, and the translation version should keep the mood. The way of choosing words in the target language becomes very important.

Anticlimax is the opposite side of climax, which can also create a rhetorical effect.

4. 2. 5   *Translation of Antithesis*

Antithesis is the rhetorical way of putting the two quite opposite phrases in a symmetrical structure.

In Antithesis, there is always an apparent contrast. By using contrast, the meaning that the speaker or writer wants to convey is more clear. And by using the contrast, the interpersonal meaning attached to the rhetoric is more easily grasped by the listener or writer. At the beginning of the long novel *A Tale of Two Cities*, the writer uses many antithesis to show the contradiction of the city. And this paragraph is one of the most famous writings in the literature history, which is partly due to this kind of rhetoric. The antithesis shows the contradiction of the society and the author's disguise towards the dark society.

Example: 横眉冷对千夫指，俯首甘为孺子牛。

One attitude is the hatred to the enemy, and the other attitude is the broad love to the partners. When these two attitudes were put together, the interpersonal meaning is expressed more clearly. The translation strategy of antithesis is to keep the contrast in the original, and the contrast in the original can help us in our choosing suitable words.

The contrast makes the viewpoint of the original text stronger, and when translators do the translation work, they should keep the contrast in the original. But the target language may not have the similar form to express the contrast meaning. Therefore, translators have to deal with this kind of structure creatively. Translators have to bear in mind that antitheses use words in pair to express the strong mood, and it is better for the translators to use pair words in the target language.

4. 2. 6   *Translation of Personification*

Personification is a kind of rhetoric that uses human being to describe other objects, producing a more vivid picture. Personification is often used in commercials and advertisements. Consumers can have a sense of closeness and they can be more easily attracted by the artistic language.

Example: Whatever it hurts, we'll heal it.

无论哪里有伤痛，我们都会治愈。

This is one sentence from the advertisement of leather bag repair service. It uses the word "heal" to express the meaning of repair. Bags are treated as something like a person. Therefore, customers will be very happy to see that their bags are carefully taken care of. Translation can keep this personification.

4. 2. 7 *Translation of Long and Short Sentences*

Simple sentences have strong emphatic function. The short sentences have a strong rhythm, which may express a series of action which happen in a short time, producing a feeling of anxiety and nervousness. The following example can show the effect that short sentences can produce.

In Ernest Hemingway's novel *Big Two-Hearted River*, he used a lot of short sentences. These simple sentences can express the light feeling of the hero after he returns from the war.

Because the short sentences also have the function of expressing interpersonal meaning, translators should catch the meaning in their context and keep this sentence form in translation.

As for language structure, there is another point that is very important and it needs to be paid attention in translation. English is characterized by hypotaxis, which means English gives more attention to the sentence structure. So formal cohesion is much emphasized. Chinese is characterized by parataxis, which means that the sentence structure is not so close, and the relation between sentence parts is often loose and not clear. This is also the reason why there are more function words in English. Chinese clauses do not use so many function words and the sentence parts are related to each other through meaning. So it is said that a Chinese sentence is like a bamboo, and the upper joint continues from a lower one, but the English is developed like a tree, with many branches extending from the stem. In translation, this kind of difference has to be paid more attention in order to present an ideal translation.

4. 2. 8   *Translation of Repetition*

To stress some kind of mood or sentiment, one particular word, phrase or sentence may be used again and again, which has a rhetorical meaning. Repetition can often be found in speech, poetry or other argumentation articles. It can attract the attention of the listener and give them a more impressive impression.

For example, in Tomas Hood's "Song of the Shirt", repetition is used as an important way to express the author's idea. In the poem, the word "work" is repeated six times. The repetition shows the hardship that the workers are enduring. By reading these repetition, readers can sense the pressure in the workers' hearts and their will to fight against the unfair treatment to them.

Generally speaking, if there is repetition in the original, we should also use repetition in the translation. For example, in translating "Song of the Shirt", in order to express the same interpersonal meaning, the same repetition should be used in the translation version. But there is some difference in this rhetorical usage. Some of the repetition in Chinese cannot have the same effect in English.

The translation doesn't use the same repetition, but it can also express the same meaning of the original. On the contrary, if translators use the same repetition with the original sentence, it would seem redundant.

In Chinese, there is always a repetition in the comparative structure, which can be seen in the following example.

Example: 这件事情条件成熟了的话可以去做,条件不成熟的话不要去做。

If the conditions were ripe it could be done, and not otherwise.

The repetition in Chinese is not translated into the same repetition in English. The only word "otherwise" can express the meaning of contrast with a simple structure. In this case, translators can use the usages according to the features of the target language. In other words, keeping the form is not so important like keeping the meaning. If the meaning can be expressed clearly without the repetition in the translation version, it can be dealt with flexibly.

On the contrary, sometimes in the translation, some elements that are not repeated in the original language have to be repeated in the target language. So the strategies in the translation of repetition are various according to different contexts. Translators can choose the suitable ways in the target language to convey the same meaning, without being restricted to by the repetition in the source language.

4. 2. 9 *Translation of Parallelism*

Parallelism can be made when phrases or sentences that have similar structures and corresponding moods are put together. Because the sentence is composed of phrases or sentences with similar structures, this rhetorical means can create the effect of foregrounding, which in turn attract the attention of the readers. In argumentation articles, parallelism will make the article's orderliness and argument clearer to the readers.

Example: And now, you who have so long been bound to the most narrow and material views, you who have denied the virtue of transcendental machine, you who have always derided your superior-behold!

喏,你这个一向目光短浅、见解鄙俗的人,你这个否认超常医学功能的人,你这个一贯嘲笑前辈的人,睁开眼睛瞧瞧吧!

4.2.10 *Translation of Rhetorical Question*

Rhetorical question is using question to express the strong positive or negative meaning. It needs no answer from the speaker or reader. In rhetorical questions, the positive form can express the strong negative meaning, and the negative form can express the strong positive meaning. Rhetorical questions can catch the attention of the listeners, and they can even make the listeners think. Then the speaker and the listeners may reach the state of resonance.

In the speech made by Patrick Henry, *Give Me Liberty or Give Me Death*, he used four continuous rhetorical questions. "*Why stand we here idle? What is that gentlemen wish? What would they have? Is life so dear, or peace so sweet, as to be purchased at the price of chains and slavery?*" The series of rhetorical questions attract the attention of the listeners and make the speech very powerful.

Let's examine another example.

Example: 在战争时期, 工程质量这样事关紧要的问题, 难道是可以争论的问题吗?

Is the quality of projects which is of vital importance the question that can be argued during war time?

The rhetorical question shows that the question is definitely not arguable, and this rhetorical usage makes the interpersonal meaning clearer to the readers.

Since the rhetorical questions show the strong feelings of speakers or writers, translators should keep this rhetorical expression. For example, in the speech made by Patrick Henry, the four rhetorical questions should use the same pattern in the Chinese version.

4. 2. 11 *Translation of Continuous Tense*

In English the interpersonal meaning can be expressed by the tense, especially the continuous tense, which can show the feeling of anger, surprise, affection or impatience, etc.

Example: Fifty-seven, his hair is just beginning to go grey.

The present continuous tense shows the feeling of surprise.

There is no corresponding usages in Chinese. So translators have to transfer the meaning with some lexical usage.

Examples: 他五十七了才开始头发变白呢。

> Paper napkins were costing the school $28.57 per case but were available at just $8.76.
> 学校为购买餐巾，每盒竟付款 28.57 美元，而其他地方价格仅为 8.76 美元。

So, Chinese can use "竟"，"竟然" or "居然" to express the feeling of surprise, use "确实"，"总算" or "倒是" to express the feeling of agreement, and use "就"，"竟"，"倒" or "到底" to express the feeling of disgust or censure.

4.3 Conclusion

People use many rhetorical expressions to make the language vivid and expressive. Different languages may have different modes of rhetoric because of the different traditions and different modes of thinking. Whatever rhetoric speakers use, it shows a kind of interpersonal meaning. So to transfer this interpersonal meaning of rhetoric appears very important. This chapter examines the usual rhetorical expressions and their strategies of translation.

The analysis of this chapter shows that many grammatical ways of expressing interpersonal meaning sometimes do not have corresponding usages in Chinese, such as the four types of moods, the modality, the subjunctive mood, the repetition and the tense. In these cases they have to be changed into lexical ways to express the interpersonal meaning. For some of the rhetoric, it is important to keep the original rhetoric if the two languages have the same usage in that kind of rhetoric. Translators can deal with the different ways of translation according to the context.

Chapter 5

Typology and the Translation of Interpersonal Meaning

5.1　The Influence of Typology on Translation Strategy

Different typology has its own contextual, text-typological and pragmatic conventions. So different typology requires different translation strategies; that is to say, different contexts call for different translation solutions. The different types of text based on communicative functions are used as the basis of translators' decisions. In her translation-oriented text typology, Katherina Reiss started to study the hypothesis that the decisive factor in translation was the dominant communicative function of the source text. This would mean that any particular text belonging to one particular text type would allow just one way of translation. Failure to recognize the text type can be a major stumbling-block in translation practice. Hatim and Mason (1990) found from the translations by the 12 translator trainees that text type was the biggest hinderance in translation practice. If translators misinterpreted text type, they would produce unsatisfying translation products. So it is one of the most important goals to recognize text action and text type in translation practice. Because the standard communication ways are used repeatedly, certain conventions can be formed in different genre conventions. Ways with the same function will be accepted as common practice in certain situations. Genre conventions are the norms that play an important role in text production. The translator should attempt to give a correct and complete representation of the source text's content and should be guided, in terms of stylistic choices made by the author, producing a certain effect on the readers. This effect is the most important element. So it has to be taken into account in translation. The stylistic choices in translation are naturally guided by those made in the source text and its context. Generally speaking, people can easily detect the differences of styles and they can also provide suitable utterance in their own culture and language. But when it comes to the foreign language, they will lack this kind of sensitivity. This requires the deep investigation of the translation theorists in this field.

Text genres are characterized by conventional features, and genre conventions play an important role in text production. The second chapter has analyzed the relation of genre and register. Then what is the strategy to analyze their role in translation? The principal criteria that turns a collection of communicative events into a genre is some shared abstract and macroscopic features. In this sense, text type can have a two-level typology. At the macro-level, genre affects the whole strategy of the text. So understanding the genres of the original text is essential to decide the global strategy in translation. At the micro-level, the individual features are determined by context of situation: field, mode and tenor. So on the lexical level or grammatical level, all the individual components of the original and the target text have to be corresponding. In fact, the most common way of recognizing text type is through the situation and the compositional features of the text. Therefore, before we translate, we have to examine the translation brief. (Nord, 1996) The translation brief contains information about the source language and the target language, the time and the place of the translation practice, the medium of the translation and the motivation of the text production.

Vocabulary and grammar are not the only things the

translators have to deal with in their translation. There are some other factors that affect the translation strategy. As to the translation of the interpersonal meaning, these factors seem even more important.

In Chapter 3, the relationship between context and meaning has already been examined, and this chapter will study how interpersonal meaning is expressed in different styles in translation. We will use some styles as examples to explain this question.

5. 2 Brief Analysis of Typology and Their Influence on Translation

Equivalence is the ideal aim in doing translation work. On the word level, translators have to use the most equivalent term between the target language and the source language. They must have the same sense on the level of tense, gender and the number of the words. On the grammatical level, it is much more difficult considering the different grammatical structure of the source and the target language. So the translators have to make changes according to the rules of target language. (Thompson, 1996) Another very important aspect is textual level. Three factors including the target audience, the purpose of the translation and the text type have a vital influence on the translator to decide what kind of tone should be used to keep the coherence in the target language. The following part will discuss the translation strategy of several text types. The first one is literary style. In this kind of text type, the translator has to consider the interpersonal meaning in the original source language, in which the author would be more likely to use lexical ways to express the interpersonal meaning. So whether the interpersonal meaning is expressed to the right point is one of the most important criteria in evaluating a translation of literary work.

5.2.1 *Literary Style*

Examples: He loathed politics, hated business, and avoided everything that might upset the even tenor of his ways.

He lived on a small income which he spend in its entirety without even touching the capital. He was quite devout, would never contradict anyone, and as he had a bad opinion of everybody he spoke well of them.

If you mentioned politics to him he would say, "I'm nothing—neither one side or the other: I don't care which party runs the government. I'm just a poor sinner who wants to live at peace with everyone."

His meekness, however, was of no avail against the finality of death. It was the only definite thing he ever did in his life.

These paragraphs are taken from a short novel. Usually novel language doesn't express the content by telling what happens, but also using the imagination of the readers. So the language must be vivid and has the function of stimulating the interest of the readers. From these paragraphs we can see that all the sentences are declarative sentences giving information to the readers, and the language can make the readers think about the hero's personality.

In this part, the interpersonal meaning is expressed by verbs, adverbs, adjectives, nouns, and even the management of these paragraphs.

(1) Declarative sentences.

(2) Verbs: loath, hate, avoid, contradict.

(3) Adverbs: ever, quite, never, only, just.

(4) Adjectives: small, devour, poor.

(5) Nouns: sinner, meekness, no avail.

(6) Management of the paragraph: Each of the paragraph is very short, and many sentences in these paragraphs are short. These short sentences and short

paragraphs give us the feeling that the author wants to tell the readers every aspect of the hero.

(7) Modality: might.

All the above mentioned methods transmit some sense of interpersonal meaning, and the reader can read the emotions of the author between the lines. So in translation, the translators should use words that can clearly show the sentiment of the original text.

Examples: 他厌恶政治、耍手腕,凡是扰乱他平静生活的一切他都躲着。

他靠这微薄的收入维持生活,花钱节俭。整个开销从不动用本金。他待人十分诚恳,从来与人无争,即使他对大家有什么看法,也尽拣好的说。

你若向他谈及政治,他总会说:"我什么都不是——既不是这一派,也不是那一派。无论哪一个党派执政我都不在乎。我只不过是一个罪人,愿同大家和平共处。"

虽然他秉性温驯,也奈何不了终有一死。这是他唯一做得很果断的事情。

Although the language is very prosaic, the author tells us about the hero with a clear sentiment, and it is this sentiment that makes the readers feel that they are very near to the hero. So when the translators translate, they have to pay attention to the interpersonal meaning of the original. From the translation we can see that there is no one to one equivalence between the source language and the target language. For example, in the first paragraph, " 凡是 , 都 " is used in Chinese to translate the word "everything" of the original text, and in the second paragraph, " 即使……也 "is used to translate the original conjunction "as". In novel style, many of the lexical meanings can show the sentiment. So the translation has to convey the sentiment meaning to the target text; that is to say, the translators should use corresponding commendatory terms and corresponding derogatory terms. Besides these features, some conjunctions can also clearly show the interpersonal meaning.

Language in novels should have the function of creating a kind of atmosphere that the readers would feel no distance with the heroes in the novel. It should try its best to create the effect that the readers are in the place where the matter happens. In English, this can be realized by using tense. Now let's look at the following example.

Example: There are no speeches, for who can speak at such a moment? A comrade advances and reads out the names of the provinces and towns represented at the funeral, the coffin is to lie on the platform until four o'clock.

It is now ten o'clock in the morning. The guards of Honor, chosen from the various factories, provinces, organizations, and regiments of the Red Army, is to be changed every ten minutes. Only the Kremlin chimes break through the silence. Then a comrade again advances and cries, "Workers of the World, Unite."

This is the description of Lenin's funeral. The author uses present tense to describe what happened in the past to create a vivid effect. It will make the readers feel that they are looking at the funeral and are deeply impressed by what happened. So in these two paragraphs, the interpersonal meaning is expressed by the finites. There are no such corresponding usages in Chinese. Therefore, Chinese has to use lexical ways to translate the interpersonal meaning which is expressed by tense in the original text.

A very important literary style is poem. The translating of poem is so hard that it is far beyond the ability of many translators. Some even argue that poems are the source language that can never be translated into a target language satisfactorily. So far from the translations, we can find that some contemporary poems have been translated either from

English to Chinese, or from Chinese to English or other languages. When translating poems, translators must bear in mind that form and sound are as important as meaning. The conveying of the ideas in the original is not enough, and the art and beauty that are expressed by certain forms and rhythms are also very important. Usually it is impossible for the translator to translate the poem into the target language using the same form, because of the quite different language structures. Translators need to make up for the loss of the meaning in a flexible way. The most important factor to decide whether it is satisfying is to see whether the original conception and style have been kept.

5. 2. 2 *Technical Style*

The biggest difference between technical style and other styles is that there are a lot of terms which are not often used in other styles. When translating this kind of text, the translators should be aware that the words in the original are usually neutral, and in the translation the corresponding terms should be chosen. These technical terms make the meaning of the articles objective and impersonal.

Example: "In offices the automation equipment used to store information, carry out computations and make routine decisions is called an electronic computer." The simplest computer once filled a room. "While processing the data, it can store 60,000 characters for reference purposes on magnetic drums like this." Now it fills your spare time. Forget that file-o-fax, instead you can carry your e-mail, your current projects, your phone numbers and your daily schedule in a palm-sized device that weighs less than 6 ounces and costs far less than the cheapest laptop. You write on the screen. The machine recognizes your writing and translates it into text. An entire industry reads the writing on the wall and translates that into money.

Hawkins figured that to succeed, his palm-sized computer would have to do four things. It would have to work faster than a proper organizer, and be able to share information with a PC. It would have to cost less than $300 and fit in a shirt pocket.

In these two paragraphs, there are few words that show any sentiment. It is just tells the readers a fact and lets the readers know some new knowledge, and it doesn't need the readers to imagine something when they read the text. So the function of this kind of style is to provide information.

Technical style doesn't show feelings or emotions in the original language. So in translation, the words that are chosen in the target language should transfer the meaning objectively, and the sentence structures in the translation are more connected than the literary style. The translation of these two paragraphs is as follows.

> "在办公室里,用来储存信息、执行计算和做出日常决策的自动化设备叫做电子计算机。"最原始的计算机曾有一间房子那么大。"当处理数据时,它可以在像这样的磁鼓里储存6万条供参考用的数据。"现在它完全占据了你的业余时间。把那些文件夹和传真机忘掉,取而代之的是,你可以把你的电子邮件、最近的工作文件、电话号码和你的日程表都储存在一个手掌大小、不足6盎司重、远比最便宜的手提电脑还要便宜的设备里。你可以在屏幕上书写,它确认你的书写并译进正文文本。整个电脑业都看准机会推出这种产品赚钱。霍金斯认为,若要成功,他的掌上电脑必须具备四个条件。那就是它的速度一定要比记事簿快,能跟个人电脑分享资讯,价钱不能超过300美元并且可以放进衬衣的口袋里。

Let's examine another example.

Example: The paper introduces the design approach of aerodynamic structure of quasi-high speed electric locomotive that is based on the foundation of conventional locomotive with the two streamlined ends. This approach has been used to the design work of several other kinds of aerodynamic structure of SS8 quasi-high speed electric locomotive. This approach is feasible since it has been proved by the data from the wind-tunnel mode.

本文介绍了以传统机车外形为基础、对机车端部适当流线化的准高速机车启动外形的设计方法,这个方法具体应用到韶山 8 型准高速电力机动车启动外形多方案设计中,最后风洞实验证明此种设计方法是可行的。

In this paragraph, there is no lexical or grammatical way to show any mood or modality. It just talked about the design of this locomotive objectively. So in the translation, translators can transfer the meaning in an objective way, without showing any emotion. And in technical style, in order to show objectivity, passive voice is often used.

5. 2. 3 *Speech Style*

Speech style can also be classified as literary style.

Here, speech style is talked separately to show its features in a clearer way. Usually facing a big audience, the speaker will choose some vocabularies which can give others a deep impression. These usages can be illustrated using the famous speech *Apology* made by Socrates.

In the speech, Socrates addressed the listeners by calling them "oh, judges". The exclamation word "oh" can emphasize his mood. He used contrast in the sentence, "no evil can happen to a good man, either in life or death after". In fact, contrast is the common way in a speech to show the speaker's feeling. "They have done me no harm, although they did not mean to do me any good." Facing death, the great philosopher was still showing his humor. Another sentence that can show the clear opposite meaning in the speech is "I to die, and you to live." Socrates used this sentence to end the speech and he was sentenced to death after the speech. Some adjectives and adverbs in the speech can clearly show the speaker's love and hate. Socrates used inverted order to show the emphasis meaning in the following sentence, "he and his are not neglected by the gods; nor has my own approaching end happened by mere chance".

In the speech, Socrates talked about death in a calm way, which showed his braveness. In the speech, he made contrast to enhance the tone. All these emotions have to be transferred in the translation version using lexical and grammatical ways. In the translation of this speech, the translator has to find the equivalent expressions in Chinese vocabularies.

5. 2. 4　*Business Letter*

Dear Sir/Madam,

　　On June 1st, we have received your letter. In the letter, you have listed the prices of the farming machinery. Since we are quite interested in this line of machinery, we often got inquiries about them from our partners in the USA. We shall be able to give you favorable orders, if the quality of the product is acceptable and the prices moderate. We shall be grateful if you like to send us some samples with the best terms and reasonable prices at your earliest convenience.

Yours truly,

In this letter, the writer used vocative "dear", adjectives "suitable, moderate, best, considerable", adverb "often" and modal operator "shall" to show the clear characteristics of the business letter. All these usages can express the politeness of the author and his wish to establish business relationship with his counterpart. All the above usages make the tone of the letter very moderate. In Chinese, we have some specific phrases that are used in letters, such as "贵","兹","谨","乞谅","收悉","承蒙","为盼". These phrases can express the respect to the counterpart and the modesty of the author. The translation of the speech is as follows.

敬启者：

贵公司于 6 月 1 日的来函已经收到。我们已获悉贵公司的农用工具价格。我公司对此类产品颇感兴趣，我方经常收到美国有关客户的来函询价，如贵公司提供的商品质量优良，价格适中，则可向贵公司大量订购。望早日收到贵公司的样品与最优惠的条件，谢谢。

谨上

5.3 Conclusion

In translation, the study of meaning is the most important basis. Translation is a dynamic process. The transfer of meaning from one language to another depends on a lot of factors. Typology is one of the important factors to affect translation. Translators have to consider the situation of the context, the purpose of the translated material when choosing the words and the tone to express the exact meaning, especially the interpersonal meaning. This chapter used literary style, technical style speech and business letter as the examples to show the importance of interpersonal meaning and the way to transfer it.

The study of meaning is the basis of translation and translation practice is by no means an easy job. It requires not only a translator who has a command of two languages, but also linguistics messages and training of translation strategies in a more serious way.

Translation is not a direct change of words from the source language to the target language. It is a craft, to some degree, an art which demands the translators' personal competence in translation professionals. (Munday, 2001) It demands linguistic skills as well as language command. It calls on the ability to make clear the distinctions, not only in the source texts to be translated, but also of the contexts, including the situation in which the translation takes place. By analyzing the differences of those text types, we can also see the importance of context. Different situations call on different translation methods on the lexical and sentence structure level and textual level. During these years, on the construction of translation discipline, the dispute whether translation is science or art has been argued for a long time. In the author's view, science or art is not so important as the method and laws of the translation practice. If we want to present satisfying translation, we should have a full knowledge of the both languages since each language has its own characteristics. Since it is possible to express the same meaning in two languages, it is also possible to convert the meaning from one language to the other. To be a qualified translator, one has to study and compare the two languages. In the study, a translator has to summarize the differences and similarities of the two languages and understand the laws behind them.

Chapter 6

Interpersonal Meaning Caused by Gender Differences

6. 1   Introduction

Over the past thirty years, and as a result of the women's movement, gender issues have become connected with the issue of language. Gender studies and language studies are both interdisciplinary academic fields. The study of language began thousands of years ago, while the study of gender is quite short. "Gender studies have developed differently, achieving the greatest influence in North America; the 'era of feminism' that began in the late 1960s and affected academic and public life as well as 'high' and popular culture has been instrumental in shaping the historical and scholarly context of its generation. Feminist work has entered and had an impact upon almost every academic discipline."(Flotow, 2004: 1)

The study of gender is important to the study of language, and the first step to study gender is to explore the difference between men and women. It is quite clear that men and women have a lot of differences in many fields. Generally speaking, women have more fat and less muscle physically; women are not as strong as men and they mature more rapidly and usually have a longer life span. Women and men often show different advantages and skills in doing their work. Why are the two genders different in so many ways? Besides some physical reasons, we are aware that social factors may account for some of the differences. For example, women may live longer than men because of the different roles they play in society and the different jobs they tend to do. Men usually have to undertake more pressure than women in life. The differences in job skills may be explained in great part through differences in the ways by which they are raised. When talking about language, we can't help asking if men and women who speak a particular language use it in different ways. If they do, then we may ask in what ways they are different. Do the differences change through time? This book attempts to explore these differences, examine the changes through time, and give these differences and changes some possible explanations.

6. 2 Male-Female Difference in Their Using Language

Language reflects, records, and transmits social differences, and we should not be surprised to find reflections of gender differences in language. Most societies differentiate between men and women in various marked ways. This book will examine the differences from the following aspects.

6. 2. 1 *Difference in Pronunciation*

Phonological differences between the speech of men and women have been noted in a variety of languages. Usually women's pronunciation is better than men's, such as the pronunciation of "-ing". Shuy(1969) made a study in this field, and he found that 62.2 % of men pronounced "-ing" in a wrong way, but only 28.9% of women didn't pronounce right. This can also be shown in the learning of a second language. Usually female students have better pronunciation than male students, and that can explain the reason why more girls choose to learn language as their major than boys. Generally speaking, girls exhibit a better ability in language.

6. 2. 2 *Difference in Intonation*

Women often like to speak in a high-pitch voice

because of physiological reason, but scientists point out that this also associates with women's "timidity" and "emotional instability". Besides the high-pitch voice, women prefer to use reverse accent as well.

Example: Husband: When will dinner be ready?

Wife: Around six o'clock.

The wife is the only one who knows the answer, but she answers her husband with a high rise tone, which has the meaning "will that do". This kind of intonation suggests women's gentility and docility. The husband will surely feel his wife's respect. Lakoff (1975) says that women usually answer a question with rising intonation pattern rather than falling intonation. In this way, they can show their gentleness, and sometimes this intonation shows a lack of confidence. On the contrary, men like to use falling intonation to show that they are quite sure of what they are saying. Falling intonation also shows men's confidence and sometimes power.

6. 2. 3 *Differences in Vocabulary*

We can notice that men and women tend to choose different words to show their feelings. For example, when a woman is frightened, she usually shouts out, "I am frightened to death!" If you hear a man says this, you'll think he is a coward and womanish.

The differences in vocabulary can be shown in the following six aspects.

(1) Color words.

There is special feminine vocabulary in English that men may not, dare not or will not use. Women are good at using color words that were borrowed from French to describe things, such as *mauve, lavender aquamarine, azure* and *magenta*, but most men do not use them.

(2) Adjectives.

In our everyday life, we can notice that women like to use many adjective, such as *adorable, charming, lovely, fantastic, heavenly*, but men seldom use them. When a woman leaves a restaurant, she will say "It's a *gorgeous* meal". If a man wants to express the same idea, he may only say, "It's a *good* meal." Using more adjectives to describe things and their feelings can show that women are more sensitive to the environment and more likely to express their emotions with words, which makes women's language more interesting than men's sometimes.

(3) Adverbs.

There are also differences in the use of adverbs between men and women. Women tend to use such adverbs as *awfully, pretty, terribly, vastly, quite, so*; men like to use *very*, *utterly*, *really*. In 1992, Jespersen found that women use more *so* than men do. For example, "It was so interesting" is often uttered by a woman.

(4) Swear words and expletives.

Maybe because women are gentle and docile, they usually avoid using swear words and dirty words. They believe that these kinds of words will not only make others uncomfortable and give an impression of "no civilization", but also destroy the relationship between themselves and others. Women always pay more attention to the grace of themselves and their use of language. We rarely hear that women utter such words as *damn*, *fuck you*, *hell*. Instead, they use *oh*, *dear* and *my god* to express their feelings.

Example: Woman: Dear me! Do you always get up so late?

It's one o'clock!

Man: Shit! The train is late again!

We can often hear similar ways of expressing shock in everyday life. Men tend to use more swear words than women. Women pay more attention to their manners and politeness of using language.

(5) Diminutives.

Women like to use words that have the meaning of "small", such as *bookie*, *hanky*, *panties*. They also like to use words that show affections, such as *dearie*, *sweetie*. If a man often uses these words, people will think that he may have psychological problem or he is not manly.

Furthermore, women like to use words that show politeness, such as *please*, *thanks*, and they use more euphemism, but "slang" is considered to be men's preference.

From the study we can see that men and women have their own vocabulary choices in achieving emphatic effects. Although in the area of vocabulary, many of the studies have focused on English, we can not deny that sex differences in word choice exist in various other languages. People need to learn to make these distinctions in their childhood.

(6) Pronouns.

Women prefer to use first person plural pronouns when they suggest something, even when she suggests the other person, while men tend to use first person singular pronoun, and when he is suggesting the other person, he will directly use the second person pronoun.

Example: Women: We need to be in a hurry.

Men: You need to be quick.

6. 2. 4 *Difference in Syntax*

Although there are no specific rules that govern

different genders to use different grammar, we can observe these differences in almost every language.

(1) Modulation.

When a woman talks, she often takes what others think into consideration. She usually leaves a decision open rather than imposes her own ideas or claims on others. We often hear a woman say *"well, you know…, I think…, I suppose…, kind of, maybe I am wrong but…,* etc."

When they want to get help from others, men and women express themselves in different ways as follows.

Example: Women: I was wondering if you can help me.

Men: Please give me a hand.

From the above example we can see men tend to ask something directly, while women tend to be more polite.

(2) Interrogative sentences.

Women use more interrogative sentences than men do. Women look interrogative sentences as a strategy of continuing a good conversation. Lakoff (1975) pointed out that compared with men, women are more likely to use an interrogative sentence to express their idea, and they like to use tag questions, because tag questions can make the tone less tense. Fishman (1980) collected many couples' conversation tapes, and he found that women used three times of tag questions as men did. In these conversations, there were 370 interrogative sentences, among which women used 263, almost two and a half of times of men did. This point is similar to the difference in intonation between men and women. Lakoff (1975) said that women might answer a question with rising tone, while men like to use falling tone to make a firm statement. According to Lakoff (1975), women tend to do this because they are less sure about themselves and their opinions than men. The different use of language also shows that women are more likely to be short of confidence. From another aspect, we can say that women are more polite and considerate than men.

(3) Imperative sentences.

A study observed a group of boys and girls on one street in Philadelphia, and the study found that the imperative sentences that the boys and girls use were different. The boys used a lot of imperative sentences but the girls used more "let's patterns".

Example: Boy: Give me an apple!

Girl: Would you give me an apple?

Boy: It's time to go.

Girl: Let's go.

The research also found that girls prefer to use

sentences with modal verbs, such as *can, could, may*. But they seldom use imperative sentences to give orders. To reduce the imperative tone, they use more adverbs like *maybe, perhaps, probably*.

(4) Correctness of grammar.

Women pay more attention to the correctness of syntax. While expressing her thoughts, she would make her utterance clear by using precise grammar.

Example: Women: We are going to go to the park today.

Men: We are gonna to the park today.

6. 2. 5 *Difference in Their Attitudes Toward Language*

Women pay more attention to using standard language than men do. So they are stricter with the rules of the use of language.

Example: Men: Are you comin'?

Women: Are you coming?

Women tend to use the standard form. This point is emphasized in the difference of pronunciation.

In Detroit, people like to use multiple negations, such as: *I do not want none*. Research found that men use much more of this kind of substandard form than women. This can be seen from movie *Forrest Gump*. Influenced by the southern accent, Forrest often uses double negative to show negative meaning.

6.2.6 *Difference in Non-Verbal Manners*

We have mentioned that women usually show politeness in their conversation, such as use of *"would you, please"*. Besides this, women also show that they are reserved when they talk. The following table is based on the research of Zimmerman and West on the interruptions men and women made in a conversation.

Table 6. 1   Interruptions Men and Women Made in a Conversation

	Male	Female	Total
Interruptions	46	2	48

We can see that men continued interrupting other's talk. Instead women are more patient. Even though they want to talk, they will wait until others stop their talking. Generally speaking, in a conversation involving both sexes, women often play the role of patient listeners. They do not interrupt others often, but encourage others to talk. However, men are eager to be heard, which pushes them to catch as many opportunities as possible. Men do not like to be silent. This makes them appear to be more active than women. In other words, in a conversation involving both sexes, women tend to be silent.

6. 2. 7 *Difference in Choosing Topics*

In social interaction, men and women have different interests in choosing their topics. When men are talking, they are more likely to choose the topics of politics, economy, stocks, sports, and current news. Women have more interest in talking family affairs, such as the education of children, clothes, cooking, fashion. Women's talk is associated with the home and domestic activities, while men's is associated with the outside world and economic activities. Thus, while there is a popular prejudice that women talk more than men, empirical studies of a number of social situations such as committee meetings and internet discussion groups have shown the opposite to be true. Women may talk more in informal occasions than men, but they surely play a second role in the formal occasions and tend to speak less than men. Sociolinguists studied women's silence in public situations as well as the linguistic work they do in their partnerships. (Spender, 1980) Besides these differences, other sex-linked differences exist. For example, women and men may have different paralinguistic system and move and gesture differently.

6. 3　Some Possible Explanations

It's not enough to find these differences. The more important thinking is to find what causes these differences. In a recent set of studies about the physical differences between the two genders, phonological processing in males is shown to be located in the left of the brain and in females to involve both left and right parts of the brain. No difference in efficiency is shown, nor is there any evidence so far that any neurophysiologic difference accounts for differences between the two groups in using language. So we can get the conclusion that the causes are social rather than physical. Since biological sexual differences cannot explain the differences in men's and women's societal roles and opportunities, scholars developed and employed other tools and analytical categories in order to understand these discrepancies. "Beauvoir suggests that a baby born with female reproductive organs does not simply grow up to be a woman. She has to turn herself into a woman, or more correctly, she is turned into a woman by society she grows up in and in response to the expectations and conditioning, and differs according to the dominant influences she is subject to in the subculture, subculture, ethnic group, religious sect, in which she grows up." (Flotow, 2004: 5) We can explore this issue from three aspects.

6. 3. 1 *Different Psychology*

It's an accepted idea that women are more careful, sensitive and considerate than men. Before a woman talks, she usually thinks of the effect her words will cause. So she often appears to be more polite. On the contrary, men appear to be rash, and they just say what they want to say and seldom care what others think. So men's speech is usually blunt and solid.

6. 3. 2 *Different Social Status*

Of the social causes of gender differences in speech style, one of the most critical is level of education. In all studies, it has been shown that the greater the differences between educational opportunities for boys and girls, the greater the differences between male and female speech. Usually, in many parts of the world, males are expected to spend longer time in schools. When offered an equal educational opportunity, there seems to be a tendency for women to be more sensitive than men to the status norms of the language.

Though many linguists have noticed the differences of usages between men and women, it was not until the 1970s that some linguists tried to find the social root of these differences. Men and women differ in the kinds of language they use and how they use it, because men and women often fill different roles in society. We may expect that the more distinct the roles are, the greater the differences. Almost in every country, most of the important positions in governments are held by men. Men can almost dominate everything. Most scholars notice that women's tone is not that self-confident as men's, and they point out that this is because they have little power or no power at all in the society. Women's social status makes them appear to be submissive to men. Women are often named, titled and addressed differently from men. For example, women are more likely than men to be addressed by their first names. Women are inferior to men in this society. So they appear to be non-assertive when they talk. They tend to discuss, share and seek reassurance. On the contrary, men tend to look for solutions, give advice and even lecture to their audience. The term gender was often understood to be the basis of women's subordination in public and private life. Women are supposed to be the second class in the household as well as in the workplace, everywhere from the pink-collar ghettos of the corporations, via images of women in the media to government or educational agencies establishing policies affecting women. Activities criticizing the gendered aspects of everyday life kept the issue in the public eye; interest and support were galvanized by media events such as the disruption of the Miss America Pageant in 1968, where the trappings of stereotypical femininity— dish-cloths, steno pads, girdles and bras—were thrown into a "Freedom Trash Can". (Morgan, 1968: 62-67)

The use of genetic masculine, such as *Everyone must increase his awareness of environment protection*, reinforces the secondary status of women in many social groups. This kind of usage does not just reflect and record current prejudices, but it is easily transmitted, reinforcing the lower power and prestige ascribed to women in a society. With the growth of social awareness in many parts of the world over the past decades, there have been many attempts to overcome this prejudicial use of language. For instance, people use the word *chairperson* instead of *chairman* more frequently nowadays. Many publishers and journals now adhere to guidelines to avoid gender stereotyping and gender prejudiced language use.

Women are very conscious about their status, and they long for a better position in society. So they try to improve themselves, including using standard language. Women are more conscious of using languages which associate with their "betters" in society, that is, those they regard as being socially superior. They therefore direct speech towards the models they provide, even to the extent in some cases of hypercorrection. On the other hand, men are powerful, including the lower-class men. They are less influenced by others.

6. 3. 3 *Different Cultural Background*

For whatever languages, there are peoples' unique life styles and modes of thinking behind them. It's these life styles and modes of thinking that make the rules of languages. Therefore, language is also a kind of cultural phenomenon. Lakoff (1975) believes that the distinction between men's and women's languages is a symptom of a problem in our culture, and not primarily the problem itself. For example, in North America, men and women come from different sociolinguistic subcultures. They have learned to do different things with language. To cite another example, the Yana language of California contains special forms for use in speech either by or to men. We can see from above that cultural background influences men's and women's behavior, including language.

6. 4 Changes Through Time

"The women's movement of the late 1960s and early 1970s tried to show how women's difference from men was in many ways due to the artificial behavioral stereotypes that come with gender conditioning. Since these stereotypes were artificial, they could be minimized." (Flotow, 2004: 8) Language has a great connection with society. So if change in society occurs, change in language, too. With the development of productive forces and civilization, the strict rules that the society prescribes for men and women are changing. Many territories do not only belong to men any more. Women are not the on-lookers; instead they begin to take a more assertive role in what goes on. For example, in a study of how the inhabitants of Observant are shifting from a pattern of stable bilingualism in German and Hungarian to the use of only German, the young girls are especially in the forefront of the language change there. Women are eager to change their social statues, and they want to be equal with men in every field. Nowadays, more and more women walk out from their homes; and even more and more of them are in the high positions in the governments. Their ability tells people that the jobs can be also done well by women. With the changes in their social status, women become more confident and assertive than before. Why should they use more euphemisms? Why should they use reverse accent even they are sure about what they say? Why should they keep silent when men are talking? They have the confidence to say what they want to say directly now.

They also have the courage to interrupt men's talk. They are brave enough to lecture to men, but not only being lectured by men. When we learn Japanese, we notice that in modern Japanese, the rules are not that strict as they were before. This is the result of modern civilization, and this is also the result women strive for.

People's linguistic behavior is not only connected with social status, but also connected with their profession, education, etc. In modern society, more and more people receive high education. We can see that more and more men begin to behave themselves when they talk. Usually, they seldom break into other's conversation abruptly. Instead they are patient enough to wait others to finish their talks. They use less rigid impressive sentences. We can hardly hear them using swear words or taboos. They become polite and gentlemen-like. The interesting thing is that they also begin to use tag questions.

6. 5　Conclusion

The differences between men and women in using language have been studied long time before. This chapter mainly discusses the differences from the aspects of pronunciation, intonation, vocabulary, syntax, manners, attitudes, and non-verbal differences in using language between men and women. Besides the differences in various aspects, this chapter tries to record the changes of these differences. On the basis of these differences and changes, this chapter also tries to make some explanation to these differences and changes.

Gender as an analytical category continues to motivate researchers in many areas. This book has seen the differences between the use of language of men and women from some aspects, and we can notice that there are many differences in using language between the two genders, and there are some changes through time. We believe that with the development of society, there will be fewer differences in the usage of language. Language, as a tool of human communication, will be improving day by day, and this needs the effort of both men and women. "The establishment of women's studies' initiatives developed from this sense of women's commonality as well as from the realization that women were excluded from large parts of public and academic life." (Flotow, 2004: 6) With more participation into the social life, business, academic field and so on, there will be other changes in the future. The changes in the language can show the improvement in women's social status.

Chapter 7

Appraisal Theory in Functionalism and Translation Evaluation

7. 1 Introduction

Communicative situations are settings in which people communicate with each other. Communication is thus a kind of interpersonal interaction. The different roles in the interaction play a significant part and thus very important in the translation process. The people involved in the communication have their own functions and roles. These roles are interconnected in a very complex network. The understanding and analyzing of these roles are very important. So sometimes action theory may be able to explain certain aspects of translation process. According to action theory, action can be defined as the change from one state of the affairs to another, mostly intentionally. In most cases, human interaction can be defined as change of a state of affairs affecting two or more people or agents. Within the same cultural background, the sender and the receiver have already formed the particular rules. Therefore, they have no difficulty in understanding each other. But when senders and receivers belong to different cultural and language backgrounds, they need an intermediary agent to bridge them. The intermediary agent needs not only the language knowledge of the source and the target languages, but also the communication rules and communication settings of both cultures.

7.2 Translation as a Form of Interpersonal Interaction

7.2.1 *The Role of Translator*

Of course, the role of the translator is vital in the whole translating process, for the translator should be responsible both for carrying out the meaning of the source language to the target language and for ensuring the result of the process. So in the process of translation, the translator first is a receiver of the source language, and then perform a translational action, which may present a short summary of the source text according to the communication setting of the target language. Translators can be compared with a target-culture text producer expressing a source-culture sender's communicative intentions. During the translation process, most of the time translators have to take receivers of the target text into consideration since the addressees of the translation is a decisive factor in the production of the target text.

7. 2. 2 *Intention and Function*

The prime principle determining any translation process is the purpose; in other words, the function of the target text is crucial to determine the word choice and tone of the translation. From the point of view of the sender, the author or the speaker of the source text wants to achieve a certain purpose, which can be called intention. (Catford, 1965) But the intention of the original source text may not achieve the ideal result, especially in the situation where the sender and the receiver are quite different. In translation, in order to achieve the function of the target text, the receiver of the translation and the purpose of the target text are the important factors to consider.

It is important to distinguish intention and function, since the sender and the receiver usually belong to different cultural and situational settings. And because of these differences of the sender and receiver, intention and function have to be analyzed from two different perspectives. The function of a particular translation task may require a free or faithful translation, or sometimes a translation between these two extremes. According to Vermeer, "every cultural phenomenon is assigned a position in a complex system of values, it is evaluated. And every individual is an element in a system of space-time coordinates. If this is accepted, trans-cultural action or communication across culture barriers has to take account of cultural differences with regard to behavior, evaluation and communicative situations". (Vermeer, 1990: 29) Two different cultural factors may be different in form, but the different forms may have the same function. The translation process involves comparing cultures. Readers who never experience foreign cultural factors themselves have to compare the foreign culture with their own cultures in order to have an understanding. So the concept of the target language culture acts as the touchstone for the conception of other cultures.

7. 2. 3 *Text Classification*

According to Reiss, text typologies help the translator specify the appropriate hierarchy of equivalence levels needed for a particular translation Skopos. Usually text types are divided according to the function the text wants to achieve, and sometimes linguistics characteristics or conventions are also important. Based on the standards, there are usually three types of texts, which are informative, expressive or operative.

In informative type, the main function of the text is mostly to tell the readers about a certain subject or phenomenon in the real world. The choice of words and phrases and the stylistic forms are all subordinate to this function. In translation of such informative type, the correct and complete representation of the source text's content is essential, and the stylistic choices should be guided by the norms of the target language and its culture.

In expressive type, the aesthetic meaning is somehow more important than informative meaning. The stylistic choices made by the author have an aesthetic effect on the reader. When translating, translators have to take this aesthetic effect into consideration, trying to present a kind of translation which can express the same interpersonal meaning in the original one.

In operative texts, both content and form are not so important compared to the extra-linguistic effect that the text is attempted to achieve. In order to bring about the same reaction to the readers or audience, sometimes the content and the stylistic features of the original text might be changed. (Bassnett, 1991)

Each text type is assumed to have many kinds of text genres, but one text genre does not always correlate with the only one text type. For example, a lover letter might be of the expressive type, a business letter would be informative, and a letter talking about complaint may belong to the operative type. So text genres are divided by conventional features, and their classification is very important in functional translation.

7. 2. 4 *Appraisal Theory*

Appraisal theory put forward by Matin is the new achievement in functional linguistics. The theory has great impact on linguistics and translation field at home and aboard. In recent years, there are lots of papers about the appraisal theory in seminars.

In *An Introduction to Functional Grammar*, Halliday has pointed out the relation between language and its function. The field of discourse, tenor of discourse and mode of discourse control the ideational function, interpersonal function and textual function respectively. (Halliday, 1985) Halliday puts more emphasis on the grammatical level, such as mood and modality. Matin also points out that lexical expressions are also the important symbols of interpersonal meaning. It is important to recognize the connection between the grammatical expressions and the lexical expressions. Usually, the lexical expressions are more concrete, since they talk about the meaning of a word or phrase in a certain context. The grammatical expressions are usually general, since it sums up the grammatical usages of mood and modality. For example, the indicative mood is used to exchange information. The imperative mood is used to exchange goods and services, and the mood mostly talks about the probability and usuality. The research about lexical expressions has a very wide range, since every word can be the research object, while the research about the grammar is comparatively smaller, since the research objects in the grammatical field are limited. But the information conveyed by the grammatical expression is much more than the information conveyed by vocabulary.

The appraisal theory is developed on the basis of functional linguistics. The most significant meaning of it is the study of interpersonal meaning in the lexical level. The study of lexical expressions makes up for the limit of research only about grammar. The appraisal theory not only expands the range of interpersonal meaning in functional grammar, but also has a great influence on language teaching, especially on the improvement of students' writing ability. The study about lexical expressions also provides the guidelines for the choices of words in translation. Translators can be guided when they are doing the translation work, and the translation work can be judged by the theory.

To evaluate translation, the ideational and interpersonal meaning should be analyzed. Whether the translation is good or not depends on the transfer of the ideational meaning and interpersonal meaning. Because the translation would certainly be influenced by the features and the cultural background of the target language, the organization of textual meaning sometimes is different with the source language. Because the two quite different systems, the difference in organization of textual meaning sometimes is necessary and this alone cannot be used to criticize the unfaithfulness of the translation.

According to the theory of functional linguistics, the language unit should be discourse. Translation, as the transfer of languages between cultures, is no exception. To describe or explain the translation process, the suitable way should take the perspective of discourse as well. The quality appraisal system of translation, which can be used to judge whether the translation is equivalent from the perspective of function, should base its theory on the discourse.

How do we judge if the target language has achieved the equivalence in ideational meaning and interpersonal meaning? According to the analysis of language behavior in functional grammar, the language people use to communicate with each other is a framework composed by form, function and context. The relation among the three is: the context determines the form, and the form becomes a kind of context as well. The form expresses function and meaning, and the function and meaning are carried out by form. The analysis of language should start from context, so does the evaluation of translation. To evaluate translation, the first step is to analyze the context and form of the source language. In this way, the meaning of the source language can be clear. In the same way, the context and meaning of the source language can be analyzed. Then whether the translation is equivalent or not with the original one is clear.

Since textual meaning is much stressed in the translation process, the central problem translation criticism focuses on the transfer of the discourse meaning of the original language, other minor factors that may also affect the transfer of meaning might be overlooked. In fact, faithfulness not only refers to the meaning of the source language, the target language, translation motivation, the application of the translation and the readers of the target language should also be the factors that are taken into consideration when evaluating the translation. If translation analysis is only based on the translation, to compare source language and target language statically is very likely to fall into a closed mechanic criticism mode, and the criticism would not be persuasive. If the analysis of translation process from the perspective of form, function and context puts the translation into the framework of all the communication factors, then the evaluation would be more reasonable. To judge whether the translation is faithful or not depends not only on textual meaning, but also on the minor factors such as the features of target language, the social and cultural environments. On the basis of these analyses, the number of places in the translation that are not equivalent can be calculated, and these data are the basis to judge whether the translation is faithful or not. The analysis based on the data is more scientific and can provide concrete ways to conduct the evaluation of the translation. From another perspective, translators can follow these guidelines to do the translation work. While doing translation work, translators always bear in mind that the minor factors such as the features of target language, the social and cultural backgrounds are all the elements to take into consideration to present an ideal translation work.

Any text consists of uncountable units of information, and these units of information are in different levels. They are different in their positions. Different languages have different language construction modes and different cultural backgrounds. So it is quite difficult to transfer the one hundred percent meaning from the source text to the target text. In other words, equivalence is impossible to achieve. The problem that translation theory needs to solve is to keep the information reduction to its lowest point. If information is not lost from the process of translating or lost as little as possible, then the meaning is transmitted to its utmost, and the translation should be the ideal one.

Since the information units are not at the same level in terms of their importance, translators' most important task is to guarantee that the main information unit that is carried by the original text should be transmitted to the target language. Even if the other information units that are in the unimportant position cannot be transmitted totally, the main information unit should be transferred clearly. In order to achieve this aim, translators must put emphasis on the whole textual meaning, instead of paying much attention to the equivalence of every word and sentence. Sometimes translators can omit, combine or reconstruct some information units that are impossible to translate. So the equivalence of the source text and the target text can be classified into two types. The first type is the necessary equivalence; that is to say, the translation must transfer the equivalent meaning in the target language, otherwise it will not be called translation. The second is the optional equivalence, the equivalence that translators choose according to the context. Which aspect should achieve equivalence, or which aspect cannot or there is no need to get the equivalence can be in the hands of translators. Because of this, different translators and different translation contexts will cause different choices. Contextual factors are important to evaluate any translation. Only on the basis of contextual factors can the evaluation be scientific and persuasive.

7. 2. 5 *Translation Criticism*

Translation criticism is one of the central subject of study in translation theory research field. Since translation evaluation is the basis of translation criticism, the research about the translation evaluation appears more important. Researchers can choose the different aspects and interest to begin their study. For example, from the research on the principles and approaches about translation theory, researchers can make a summary about the present study in this field and arrive at the conclusion on the level of philosophy. On the other hand, researchers can choose a certain type of text and make evaluation just on the certain type. This can be classified into the study of translation practice rather than the study of theory. But to make a scientific study, both the theory field and the practice field are important. However, some of the parameters in this book are not so scientific and the procedures are too simple, and the whole assessment system has only the upward direction. Moreover, Reiss' study is based on the translation of English to German. To apply it into the translation of English to Chinese is not so reasonable.

Since too many factors have to be taken into consideration to evaluate translation work, it is very hard to render a scientific and comprehensive system. To construct a comprehensive, scientific and practical evaluation system is even more difficult. Although there are many studies about this field, the result is not that satisfying. In German translation theorist House's *Translation Quality Assessment*, she used the theories on functional linguistics and discourse analysis to analyze the eight types of English to German translation. She presented a set of comparatively scientific system and procedure. It is the first translation assessment system and starts the research in this field.

Taking equivalence as her basis, Reiss develops a model of translation criticism based on the functional relationship between source and target texts. According to Reiss, the ideal translation would be one "in which the aim in the target language is equivalence as regards the conceptual content, linguistic form and communicative function of a source language text. She refers to this kind of translation as integral communicative performance." (Nord, 2001: 9)

Reiss herself is an experienced translator, having finished many translations from Spanish into German. From her own translating experience, she found that real life sometimes gives situation where equivalence is not possible, and in some cases, the equivalence is not desired. In many situations, it is impossible for translators to offer the same amount and the same kind of information as the source-text can produce. Translators will use another form to offer another kind of information. Translators have their own assumption of the readers, or audiences need, expectations, or the knowledge they already have, and so on. The new assumptions made by the translators must be different from those made by the original writers, since the source language addressees and the target language addresses are in quite different cultures and language communities. So equivalence is definitely not the only and feasible standard to do the criticism in translation work. This view directly challenges the traditional concept of equivalence as the standard of translation. For the occasion that equivalence is not desired, the reason is that the target text is intended to achieve a purpose or function other than that of the original, such as adapting a prose text for the stage, translating Shakespeare's plays for foreign-language classes, or providing word-for-word translations of an Arabic poem intended to serve as a basis for a free rendering by an English poet who does not know the source language. A further exception is when the target text addresses an audience different form the intended readership of the original text.

7. 2. 6 *Intentionality, Acceptability and Informativity*

Communication has certain intention to achieve. The speaking and writing in its context convey a kind of intention the speaker or writer wants to fulfill, such as making an order or request, expressing certain feeling. This is called intentionality in the discourse level. From the relation of function and form, different functions require different forms to convey the meaning. For example, greeting, making a declaration, or presenting a speech have quite different forms. On the other hand, from the perspective of the relation between textual structure and intentionality, the differences are apparent. The relation between discourse structure and intentionality in instruction pamphlet, patent book or legal regulations is more direct, while in some literary styles, such as in poems, the discourse structure and the intention the poet wants to express is not that clear. From the perspective of communication process, language realizes its function through the coding and decoding between the sender and the receiver and intentionality is the term from the angle of the speaker or writer. To understand the intentionality would certainly help the better transfer of meaning in translation.

Acceptability is a term from the angle of the receiver. If the intention of the speaker or writer in the original text cannot be decoded and accepted by the receiver, then the communication will fail. So in order to make the communication smooth, the discourse made by the sender must be acceptable and can be decoded by the receiver. Sometimes because of the complexity of context and social differences, the intention accepted by the receiver may not be the same as the intention the sender wants to convey.

Informativity is another important nature in discourse analysis. Informativity means the content, information and knowledge the discourse conveys. If the content in the discourse is totally new to the receiver, then the degree of informativity is high, and the receiver may have greater interest; otherwise, the interest may be low. But if the informativity is too high, that is to say, the receiver has a lot of difficulty in understanding it, then the readability is low. Translators should take this into consideration. To make the translation which has high informativity readable and understandable, translators have to add some explanation in the notes or provide the reader some background information.

7. 2. 7 *Translation Errors*

According to the theory of functionalism, the notion of translation error must be defined in terms of the intention of the text and translation process. Error means the meaning of the original text is not expressed in the target text. Errors can be classified into such types as offense against the function, or against the coherence, or against the text type or not in accordance with the cultural conventions. "A particular expression is not adequate in itself; it only becomes adequate with regard to the communicative function it was supposed to achieve." (Nord, 2001: 73) Knowledge about error and error type can help training translators. According to the study, students make fewer linguistic mistakes if they know clearly the situation for which they are translating. If translators don't know the purpose of translating, they will be confined to the source-text sentence structure. In other words, they have no clear direction towards the target text. The less they know about the intention of the translation, the more likely they make mistakes. Knowing the situation and cultural factors in the target language is important, and the knowledge of translators'own cultural background is even more important. Because if we want to translate in an adequate way, there must be certain type of comparison between the two languages and cultures. "To do this, we have to replace our intuitive behavior patterns with conscious knowledge of our cultural specificity." (Nord, 2001: 79)

7. 3 Conclusion

The function of language is to communicate. So meaning is the most important concept. In the field of translation, the conveyance of meaning is the only goal. To transfer the meaning in a more scientific way is the topic many translators and translation theorists try to explore. This chapter is using theories of functionalism to explore the subjects of translation criteria and translation evaluation. Using the theories of functionalism, the study of translation theories appears more scientific.

Meaning is probably the most complex term in

linguistics, and because of the complexity of meaning, the nature of translation becomes difficult to define. It has been proved through the history that the theory about meaning in functionalism is more scientific than other schools. It divides meaning into three parts and every part has its own system. This book takes the interpersonal meaning as the subject of study.

In functional linguistics, the study of meaning serves for the analysis of discourse. A successful discourse has to accomplish two tasks. The first one is to find the right form to express the meaning. As to the interpersonal meaning, it is to choose the suitable ways to express the sentiment or attitude of the speaker or writer. The second is that the choices should be defined by the contextual factors. The first task is the internal requirement and the second one external requirement. The theory of functionalism is more scientific than the theory of formalism because it pays more attention to the contextual factors. Translation is closely connected to discourse. So a successful translation should also accomplish the two tasks: first, it should meet the internal requirement of meaning, and second it should also meet the external requirement of context. Translation is the transmission of language meaning in use, and the study of translation should adhere to the environment the language is in. Context is one of the crucial factors to decide the translation strategy.

The nature of translation and the nature of the functional linguistics have some agreements on their attention of context, and in recent years, many scholars have applied the theory of functional linguistics to the theory of translation. This book also tries to connect the functional linguistics with the translation theory.

On the basis of the structure given by functional linguistics, the author has explored the mood system and modality system of English and Chinese and finished the researches on the topics "Typology and the Translation of Interpersonal Meaning" "Lexical Ways of Expressing Interpersonal Meaning and Translation Strategy" and "Rhetorical Ways of Interpersonal Meaning and Translation Strategy". By studying the interpersonal meaning in English and Chinese, the similarities and differences between the two languages can be found, and this is helpful to the translation. In the papers, the author tries to explore the relation between typology and interpersonal meaning. It takes some styles as examples, and tries to get the conclusion that different styles and different intentions of the original texts have different ways of expressing interpersonal meaning. Therefore, this requires translators to fully understand the type and its intention before translating. The insight into the relationship of form and function becomes the basic procedure in the interpersonal analysis of discourse within the theory of register. Text typology involves genre analysis, which can help the translators develop strategies that facilitate their work and provide satisfactory translation.

Bibliography

[1] Bassnett, S. *Translation Studies (Revised Edition)* [M]. London: Longman, 1991.

[2] Bassnet, S. & Andre, L. *A Preface to Contemporary Translation Studies* [M]. London: Routledge, 1998.

[3] Benjamin, A. *Translation and the Nature of Philosophy: A New Theory of Words* [M]. London: Routledge, 1989.

[4] Catford, J. C. *A Linguistic Theory of Translation* [M]. London: Oxford University Press, 1965

[5] Firth, J.R. *The Technique of Semantics* [M]. Oxford: Oxford University Press, 1935.

[6] Halliday, M.A.K. *An Introduction to Functional Grammar* [M]. Beijing: Foreign Language Teaching and Research Press, 2000.

[7] Halliday, M.A.K. & Hasan, R. *Language, Context and Text: Aspects of Language in a Social-Semiotic*

Perspective[M]. Geelon: Deakin University Press, 1985.

[8]　Hatim, B. & Mason, I. *The Translator as Communicator*[M]. London: Routledge, 1997.

[9]　Hatim, B. & Mason, I. *Discourse and the Translator*[M]. Shanghai: Shanghai Foreign Language Education Press, 2001.

[10]　Hewson, L. and Jacky, M. *Redefining Translation*[M]. London & New York: Routledge, 1991.

[11]　Katherine, R. *Translation Criticism*[M]. Melbourne: Deakin University Printery, 1989.

[12]　Long, Huang. *Translatology*[M]. Nanjing: Jiangsu Educational Publishing House, 1987.

[13]　Malinowski, B. *Coral Garden and Their Magi*[M]. London: Allen & Unwin, 1946.

[14]　Martin, J.R. & Rose. *Working with Discourse*: *Meaning Beyond the Clause* [M]. London: Continuum, 2003.

[15]　Newmark, P. *Approaches to Translation*[M]. Oxford: Pergamon Press, 1981.

[16]　Nord, C. *Text Analysis in Translation*[M]. Amsterdam: Rodpi, 1991.

[17]　Nord, C. *Translating as a Purposeful Activity*[M]. Shanghai: Shanghai Foreign Language Education

Press, 2001.

[18] Reiss, K. Text Type, Translation Types and Translation Assessment[A]. In Chesterman, A. (ed.) *Readings in Translation Theory*[C]. Helsinki: Oy Finn Lectura Ab, 1989.

[19] Tosborg, A. *Text Typology and Translation*[M]. Philadelphia: John Benjamin's Publishing Company, 2000.

[20] Vermeer, H. J. *Quality in Translation*[M]. Lewven: Katholieke Universititeit, 1990.

[21] 陈宏微. 汉英翻译基础 [M]. 上海: 上海外语教育出版社, 1998.

[22] 金惠康. 跨文化交际翻译续编 [M]. 北京: 中国对外翻译出版公司, 2004.

[23] 李红宇. 文化语境与翻译连贯 [J]. 重庆交通大学学报, 2014(10): 67-69.

[24] 李亚舒, 黄忠廉. 科学翻译学 [M]. 北京: 中国对外翻译出版公司, 2004.

[25] 李忠华. 韩礼德翻译研究评述 [J]. 北京科技大学学报, 2013(4): 123-125.

[26] 汪国瑜. 科技翻译中的逻辑思维 [J]. 中国翻译, 1984(2): 68-70.

[27] 夏秀芳. 英汉人际意义的表达及翻译策略 [J]. 商业文化, 2011(11): 98-99.

[28] 张春柏. 英汉汉英翻译教程[M]. 北京：高等教育出版社, 2003.

[29] 张惠君. 商务英语翻译原则探讨[J]. 东北电力大学学报, 2006(5)：86-89.

后　记

　　目前在功能语言学的研究中,研究者已经把目光从对语篇内容和形式的研究,也就是对概念意义和语篇意义的探索,转向对人际意义的研究。对人际意义的探索已经吸引了各个领域的学者的目光,包括哲学家、语用学家、社会语言学家和系统功能语言学家,其中系统功能语言学家的贡献最大。人际功能是功能语言学家韩礼德提出的三大语言元功能之一,另外两项功能分别为概念功能和语篇功能。韩礼德认为人际功能和人际意义是两个可以互换的概念。人际功能指的是语言除了传递信息之外还具有表达讲话者的身份、地位、态度、动机等功能。通过这一功能,讲话者使自己参与到某一情景语境中来表达态度,并试图影响和改变他人的态度和行为。国内外从功能语法角度对人际意义的研究已涉猎到很多体裁,如广告、学术论文、新闻、自传、总统的演讲词等,也包括在翻译时如何对等地翻译出原文的人际意义。

　　翻译是不同语言之间意义的传递,所以翻译理论的研究必须以意义的研究成果为基础,同时对翻译的研究也能够促进对意义的进一步探索。

功能语法中人际意义是由语气、情态和语法隐喻来表达的。笔者在学习和研究中发现人际意义除了这几种表达方式之外,还有其他多种表达方式,例如,具有感情色彩的词汇表达法,具有情感意义的修辞表达法以及其他方式。通过对表达人际意义的各种方式的探索,有利于在阅读、翻译时更好地把握字里行间流露出的情感。在此基础上探讨各种翻译策略,能够使译者在翻译时准确传递意义,力求达到翻译的忠实标准。

翻译理论已经不再一味追求原文与译文的所谓对等,而是在研究语境和翻译目的的基础上,探讨翻译的策略。系统功能语言学为翻译提供了可行的理论依据。根据系统功能理论,翻译不可能脱离语境。交际功能观把原文文本、文体以及翻译所要达到的目的有机地结合在一起,对译者把握全文,正确理解原文,顺利完成翻译起到积极有效的作用。因此,功能理论注重对翻译活动中其他因素的研究,比如译文的读者、译文的用途等。总之翻译时很强的目的性作指导,这给传统的翻译理论研究带来了新思路。

建立在功能语言学基础上的翻译策略摆脱了传统的以文本为中心的等值观的束缚,把研究的重心转移到了意义以及文体和翻译的目的上,同时兼顾了语言与文化两个方面。译者有权根据翻译目的以及译文在译语文化里要实现的功能调整其翻译策略,从而充分发挥译者的能动性。

笔者要特别感谢邓红风教授和张德禄教授。在1999—2002年间,笔者在中国海洋大学攻读硕士学位时,在张德禄教授的课堂上开始接触功能语言学理论,并且在导师邓红风教授的指导下,将功能语言学理论知识和翻译理论结合起来。李战子教授有关人际意义的论述给本书提供了理论指导。她对人际意义的表达方式脱离了韩礼德教授的语气和情态,思维更为开拓,笔者从中受到很多启发。本书不仅将系统功能语言学的理论知识作为翻译实践的基础,而且用系统功能语法的评价理论来评价翻译,该理论为翻译批评提供了方向和理论基础。自2002年起笔者开始从事大学英语教学,课堂上的教学实践为本书提供了素材,也非常感谢青岛科技大学的领导和同事给予的支持。当然,所有的成果都离不开家人的支持,非常感谢丈夫法永刚的支持和理解,感谢儿子法竣译能够在生活和学习上独立,给予笔者足够的时间完成本书。

夏秀芳

2016 年 6 月